WITH LOVE, FROM

Cynthia ♡

A collection of recipes & remembrances

BY CYNTHIA COLLINS PEDREGON The Peach Tree Gift Gallery and Tea Room FREDERICKSBURG, TEXAS

BOOK DESIGN BY
Susie Hiskey Bryan

PHOTOS BY
James Fox
© 1999 James Fox

PHOTO STYLING
Tina, Helana and Cynthia Pedregon

MODELS
Claire and Rose Pedregon: tea, salad and cookies
Lydia Castillo: bread and cosmos

Copy © 1999
Peach Tree Gift Gallery & Tea Room
210 South Adams Street
Fredericksburg, Texas 78624
(830) 997-9527

1st Printing   10,000 copies

ISBN 0-9627590-1-5
Library of Congress Catalog Card 99-075258

cookbook resources
541 Doubletree Drive
Highland Village TX 75067
(972) 317-0245

A Prelude to the Feast

ALL ONE NEEDS TO DO IS LOOK AND WALK
through our gift selections to realize that I don't do well limiting
my buying to one line of soap or one style of home accessory!
There is so much in life to celebrate and experience…
for example, breakfast with friends, popcorn and Cokes with
Hector when we escape to the movies, early morning work outs
with Tina including the occasional secret donut. Then there are
lobster feasts with David and Helana in Boston, cookies and chocolate and pretend tea with my sweet Claire and Rose, Collins
Chocolate Cake at every family birthday feast… pot luck lunches
at church and picnics with my girls to celebrate the bluebonnets.
The list goes on … memories and hugs and tears when someone
you love with all your heart makes his entrance to heaven for the
eternal feast…

The Journey

THIS BOOK HAD ITS BEGINNINGS ABOUT FOUR YEARS ago after Tina and I completed our second book, **The Peach Tree Family Cookbook.** I knew I had more to say, and the more I directed my thoughts to the content, the more I felt I should give emphasis to a book on living a healthy life style especially concerning food.

A healthy lifestyle was not a new idea to me. Growing up, soft drinks were for very special occasions only — my parents made their own yogurt — we had our own chickens — and later when I was caring for my own family, I was diligent to provide foods that were nutritious for them — carefully avoiding so much of the preserved, prepared foods that began flooding the market at that time. I bought whole milk from a local dairy, made my own breads — sometimes my own butter — and enjoyed being part of a natural foods co-op with a group of like-minded friends. I have always preferred making meals using fresh whole foods — preferring them to overly processed foods. I carried this same concept over to our serving ethics in the Tea Room Restaurant. It's extremely important to me to use the very best and freshest ingredients available to serve those who come under our roof.

During the early stages of this book I began to wonder if I were overly concerned with food. My faith as a Christian is so important to me that more than anything I have a desire to please my Lord.

I felt that to write a book concerning healthy lifestyles would require complete honesty and perhaps vulnerability on my part. I began to look more deeply at myself and to ponder what was positive — and what needed to be pushed away. I began a remarkable journey that I'm still experiencing and traveling — a time of reflection and reassessing. Hector and I were entering a new season in our lives, both of us needing to shed some weight — to commit more seriously to the disciplines of regular exercise.

In the spring of 1995, I was asked to speak to a women's group in a San Antonio church. I have always been very uncomfortable speaking publicly, but I consented to give my story. The gift I received in putting myself through the experience of preparing for the talk was my biggest surprise. I spoke about the need we all have to discover our niche — we all desire to be significant and to make an impact, and we all have within us something unique with which to reflect God's love and creativity.

The idea of a healthy lifestyle began to develop for me with new and fresh insights. I came to a place where I could believe with confidence that food itself is not the enemy. Any problem I have concerning food directs me to my attitude. There are times when I still struggle and get out of balance — mending my heart with food - going to the kitchen when I should be going on my knees. At these times food has often let me down — only to show my need for intimacy with our loving heavenly Father.

It didn't happen instantly, but since that speaking experience I have felt an amazing discovery and release within myself to feel real joy and gratefulness that God has indeed gifted me with talents concerning the preparation and serving of food to others. Instead of the guilt that occasionally gnawed at me, I began to relax and rest knowing how good God is to allow me to spend my time — and career — doing what I love to do. I relate to the scene in the movie, Chariots of Fire, when Eric Liddel said to his sister, Jenny — "When I run, I feel His pleasure."

The kitchen has been a place of comfort and a haven for me as far back as I can remember. It is the center of my home. I am drawn to it. It is where I so often discover answers when I'm confused, and comfort when I have been hurt. It's where I invite my friends to sit with me — it's where I'm reminded in my quiet times how good God is, and how blessed I am to know of His love.

It's not surprising to think that being in my kitchens, and teaching cooking classes, has been a part of my healing process after the sudden loss of our precious and beautiful son, Carlos in June of 1996. My life seemed so easy until that terrible day. Yes, I'd experienced losses — my parents both died suddenly — but somehow that didn't seem totally out of God's perfect order.

It is part of growing up to know that your parents will precede you into eternity. Losing Carlos has so changed our lives — made our whole world different — and I live with the hard pain of knowing that my life will not be perfectly right ever again.

Losing our son totally depressed us — broke our hearts and for a time all energy we had was given over to survival only. I then put the cookbook on hold for a time.

Comfort food took on a new meaning as I spent time in the kitchen which has always been a place of comfort and creativity for me. As I cooked in the Tea Room kitchen, the time I spent working with bread or over the stove became more meaningful for me. I have so many good memories of cooking with Carlos in both the Peach Tree kitchen and in our home kitchen.

As days and months came and went, I felt a new strength filling me — and a deep joy centered around all my surfacing memories of being a mother to such a precious son - and the awareness of the wealth of rich relationships and friends that surround me. At the same time that I had lost a son, I also became a grandmother to our beautiful little Claire, and now Rosemary Grace. I had an awareness of all of the loved ones around me that I could nurture around my table. Thus, I began to write again with new enthusiasm for this book.

I have had a growing passion in these last three years to share what I'm learning through this dreadful pain. We must all consider how we are to define our healthy lifestyle. There is a time for low fat cooking and exercising my muscles — but at the core of it all, for me, it is the relationship with those God has given me to know and love with Him.

Food, prepared well and beautifully served is the vehicle God has given me to bring those I know and love closer to one another. Preparing food with friends and family is where I have some of my favorite conversations and happy memories. For me it's around the table — sharing hearts, grief, laughter, tears… Kleenex. Yes, for me it's around the table — at the heart of the home - that miracles happen.

It's around the table that miracles happen!

WHEN I THINK OF MY MOTHER'S COOKING, one of my favorite memories as a little girl was waiting for her home-made bread to come out of the oven. Mom would remove it from the oven and spread a pat of butter all over the top to make the bread glisten. Then she would slice some bread, butter it, and let us drizzle honey all over it. Was that good! Nothing like it! The smell and taste of fresh baked bread hot from the oven is hard to beat.

My parents share a passion for family. It has been important to them that David, Carlos, and I be a part of all that they do. I remember the tennis games — we were just little kids at the time, but they made us feel important by letting us "work as ball boys", retrieving tennis balls as they needed them.

Mom was really busy when she opened the Tea Room. After walking home from school, we would check in with her and pick up a snack while we talked about our day. She wanted the Tea Room to feel like home for us. One way she did this was to have ice cream pie on the menu which was always a treat for us at home.

At the start of the Tea Room years ago, David, Carlos, and I knew how to do everything from waiting tables and cooking to washing dishes and mopping. One of our favorite early Tea Room memories was that of waiting tables, just the three of us with Carlos' buddy, Shawn Martin. We would spend the whole day working with Mom in the kitchen and with Dad in the gift shop. We all knew we were going to work hard but were content because we knew we would have a good time together.

We always depended on David to be in charge and he was comfortable in that role. Carlos and Shawn were given the duties of mopping and hosing off the mats from the kitchen at the end of each day. This was a gruesome task, but hilarious to see which one could con the other into doing the job alone. The winner usually walked by grinning triumphantly, saying something clever like, "how does the soap taste", or "only ten more to go." At this point, the winner had to take off running since the loser aimed a water hose on full blast.

Since my little brother's tragedy, our family bond has only grown stronger. It is evident in the ways we make time for each other and in ways we listen to each other more. There is a sensitivity that has grown stronger. We now have a greater desire to be more present in each others lives in ways that are important. That is why it is no surprise that we have supported Mom in different ways in the writing of her third cookbook. One surprise was David's interest in cooking and his sending a recipe that he created for Mom's book. David has always enjoyed Mom's cooking but has recently shown more interest in cooking and entertaining in his own home.

On the other hand, Carlos loved to be in the kitchen. He loved cooking and entertaining. I have met very few people who have a good time in the kitchen cooking only for themselves. He could easily put something tasty together out of a few simple ingredients. Before we served breakfast in the Tea Room, Carlos would go into the Tea Room kitchen, take a tour through all the refrigerators, and cook a wonderful breakfast for himself. He would have everyone working in the kitchen salivating over his meal.

In many ways, this book is like an heirloom for our family because there are so many memories throughout the book which have meaning for us all. Even though Carlos' name is only on a few pages, his presence is throughout the book. His life was one of many adventures, relationships, and celebrations. We have great memories of Carlos, singing and playing his guitar and harmonica at the table after dinner — he was quite a storyteller.

In the dedications in the Peach Tree Tea Room cookbook, Mom wrote that God was faithfully showing her that "all things work together for good to those who love Him and are called according to His purpose". Our family is beginning to understand the wisdom of this verse through celebrating Carlos' life. We savor wonderful meals together — we celebrate more often— we enjoy each other as the gifts that we are and in this way — "ALL THINGS work together for GOOD to those who LOVE HIM."

From My Heart

My thanks to the many folks (or many of you) whom we've yet to meet, but who sent love and blessings and encouragement to us when we lost Carlos, simply because you know us through our books and chose to share our pain — you are truly Peach Tree family — Bless you!

Bless you **Loretta Schmidt** for all of the typing of this book — entering all my recipes and thoughts into our computer (which I've yet learned to turn on) and for all the sweet moments you sat with me so totally present as I opened the bitter sweet places in my heart.

To **Susie Hiskey** and **Jim Fox** for giving the extra ingredient of love and perception added in with their brilliant design talents that has given me unexpected joy in this incredible book writing experience!

To the **Peach Tree staff** for shouldering more of the load so I could focus my time on writing this book.

Thanks to **Peggy Cox** for all the great times together in my kitchen testing, tasting and perfecting each recipe.

Many thanks to **Ken Gire's** words of encouragement in his retreat early this spring: "I love revisions, where else can spilled milk turn into ice cream."

For my close circle of friends — my treasures in earthen vessels — with whom I can laugh, grieve, rejoice and be whatever I need to be that day — and some, who though I don't see them often are a very necessary thread that holds my life together.

To **Katie Bess** — whose example and teaching has given me a picture of how a healthy life style looks — and the encouragement to trust in God's goodness and his direction for my ultimate good.

Blessings to my **Aunt Mella** for her grand editing skills, and the days of sitting with these recipes, and reading and editing to perfection.

To **Hector** — joy is having you next to me in this journey we're traveling together

Thank you **Tina**, **Helana** and **David** for the blessings of support you give me continually.

All things come of thee O Lord —
and of thine own have we given thee

living relationship

Dedicated to my son

C A R L O S

1972-1996

Being his mother has changed

and brightened my life forever...

...and hence this book.

to

Hector, Tina, David, Helana, Claire and Rose,

I celebrate you—

contents

My way of cooking

ONE OF MY HEARTFELT MESSAGES IS TO COMMUNICATE MY way of cooking. If you will notice throughout this book, I have listed options with so many of the recipes.

This is the real me in the kitchen! I am constantly on the lookout for new recipes and forever changing, revising, blending whenever I discover a new idea or taste a new dish that I've not had before.

Some of you may want the security of having it all measured out for you, and that is wonderful, too. There is so much to do in our busy lives and each one of us has our special God-given area of gifting. I realize that not everyone has such a passion for creative cooking, which is so much a part of my story — I love to eat good food! Serving good food to others is one of the ways I share myself. It's my offering — my blessing.

breakfast

muffin notes

THE INSTRUCTIONS FOR OUR MUFFINS CALL FOR FILLING the muffin pans two thirds full in order to produce the standard size muffin. For the giant muffins we make in the Tea Room we use a large ice cream scoop to fill the muffin pans to the top. During baking the batter flows up and over the edges forming a beautiful large crown. We have learned that it is most helpful to grease lightly the entire pan - top and all — you will have beautiful big muffins and they can easily be removed from the pan with their edges intact! You will need to add some baking time because of added batter.

FINISHING TOUCHES - PRETTY AND DELICIOUS!
dip warm muffins in a little melted butter, then in granulated sugar for brilliant sparkle

FOR A DAB OF MAPLE GLAZE ON TOP — Mix together 3 cups powdered sugar, 1 tablespoon maple syrup, 1-1/2 teaspoons vanilla, 2 tablespoons butter, 2 tablespoons milk (or more if needed to make it creamy and spreadable) and drizzle over muffins. This makes 1-1/2 cups.

GIANT ORANGE WALNUT TEA ROOM MUFFINS

lemon delight muffins

Tina likes to begin her morning with a giant homemade muffin —
When we're at home the Orange Walnut is her choice, but when we
travel, we love to search out new bakeries for our breakfast. On one
such trip she enjoyed a very light lemony muffin. My challenge
from Tina has been to bake a lemon muffin just like the one she
remembers, and this is it. Only she says this one is even better!

2 cups unbleached flour
I teaspoon baking powder
I teaspoon soda
1/4 teaspoon salt
1/4 cup sugar
2 tablespoons honey
2 eggs
I-1/4 cups plain yogurt, room temperature
1/4 cup butter, melted
2 tablespoons lemon juice
Zest of I lemon

❶ Preheat oven to 350 degrees. Grease muffin tins.
❷ Combine flour, baking powder, soda and salt. Set aside.
❸ In another bowl, combine remaining ingredients.
   Add dry ingredients and mix.
❹ Fill muffin tins to two thirds full.
❺ Bake for 15 minutes or until wooden toothpick in center
   comes out clean.

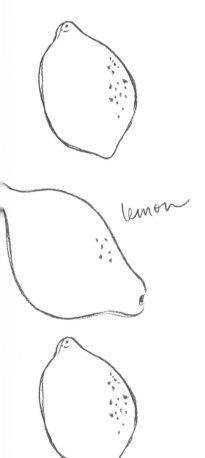

lemon

Lemon syrup:
2 tablespoons lemon juice
1/3 cup powdered sugar

Combine ingredients mixing well so there are no lumps.
Drizzle over warm muffins.

Makes 12 muffins.

VARIATION:

INSERT A CHUNK

OF CREAM CHEESE,

APPROXIMATELY 2 TO 3

TEASPOONS, INTO TOP

OF BATTER WHEN

FILLING TINS.

NOTE:

THIS BATTER CAN BE

STORED IN THE REFRIGER-

ATOR FOR UP TO 10 DAYS.

big bran muffins with raisins and dates

I made the most wonderful discovery when we were preparing our breakfast menu in the Tea Room. Muffin batter can be mixed the day before it is to be used! What a great way to start the morning whether you're preparing for your family or friends — or as in our case, sometimes an army!

2-1/2 cups unbleached flour
1-1/2 tablespoons baking soda
1 tablespoon baking powder
2 teaspoons ground cinnamon
1/4 teaspoon salt
3/4 cup vegetable oil
2 tablespoons maple syrup
1/4 cup molasses
1 cup light brown sugar, firmly packed
1 teaspoon vanilla extract
3 large eggs, lightly beaten
2 cups buttermilk
1 cup wheat germ
1 cup natural bran (not cereal)
1/2 cup dates, plumped with scalding water, drained, and coarsely chopped
1 cup dark raisins, plumped with scalding water and drained.

❶ Whisk first 5 ingredients together in a medium bowl; set aside.
❷ In a large bowl, whisk next 5 ingredients together. Blend in eggs, then buttermilk, wheat germ, and bran. Let batter rest 10 minutes.

3 Whisk dry ingredients into wet mixture to blend partially.
   Continue mixing batter with a rubber spatula, making sure
   that ingredients at the bottom are incorporated into batter.
   Fold in dates and raisins.

4 Cover batter with plastic wrap and refrigerate at least
   1 hour, preferably overnight.

5 In a preheated 400 degree oven, adjust oven rack
   to middle position.

6 Spoon into greased muffin tins.

7 Bake until tops brown, about 20 minutes.
   (If not done after 20 minutes, reduce temperature
   to 350 degrees and bake until muffins are done.)

Makes 22 muffins.

sticky gooey cinnamon rolls

I acquired this treasure of a recipe when Martha Kipcak married John Hughes. Martha gave me her recipe so we could serve these delicious rolls at her lovely garden wedding reception. It added a personal touch to a precious family celebration, and now we are blessed to share in the tradition!

Yeast dough:
1 tablespoon yeast
2 tablespoons sugar
1/4 cup warm water
1 tablespoon salt
1/4 cup sugar
2 cups hot water
1/3 cup shortening
1 egg, lightly beaten
6 cups unbleached flour, divided use

1. Dissolve yeast and 2 tablespoons sugar in 1/4 cup warm water and let stand 5 minutes.
2. In another bowl, dissolve salt and 1/4 cup sugar in 2 cups hot water.
3. Add shortening to the salt-sugar mixture and beat until smooth.
4. Add egg, 2 cups flour and yeast mixture to shortening mixture and beat until smooth.
5. Add 2 more cups flour and beat again.
6. Add remaining 2 cups flour, working dough until all flour is moistened.
7. Place dough in greased bowl, turning to coat on all sides.
8. Cover with plastic wrap and let rise in refrigerator overnight.

Sauce:

3/4 cup butter
1-1/2 cups brown sugar
3 tablespoons half and half
1-1/2 cups pecans, chopped

Filling:

1/2 cup butter, melted
1/2 cup sugar
1/4 cup ground cinnamon

Next day:

1. In large sauce pan, melt butter. Add brown sugar and half and half; bring sauce to a simmer.
2. Pour sauce into two 9 x 12-inch pans and sprinkle with pecans.
3. Remove dough from refrigerator and divide into two parts.
4. Roll each part into a long rectangle about 12 x 18 inches. Spread with melted butter.
5. Mix sugar with cinnamon and sprinkle over dough.
6. Roll up dough from the long side like a jelly roll. Slice into 1-inch slices.
7. Place slices on end in prepared pans. Cover, and let rise until doubled in bulk, about 1 hour.
8. Bake at 375 degrees for 20 to 25 minutes or until golden brown.
9. Remove from oven and invert immediately onto cookie sheet or platter. Serve warm or at room temperature.

Makes 24 rolls.

breakfast scones

This is the recipe for the giant scones which we serve in the Tea Room. We've also used small heart cutters to make them petite for teatime parties. Every time I make these scones I remember the woman in the TV commercial giving instructions for her prize biscuits, "I'm careful not to overwork the dough!" That is an important key to success with this recipe. Using a light hand in mixing and forming the scones will reward you with lighter scones!

4 cups unbleached flour
2 teaspoons cream of tartar
I teaspoon baking soda
I teaspoon salt
4 tablespoons sugar
8 tablespoons butter, chilled and cut into I/2-inch pieces
I cup golden raisins
I-I/2 cups milk
I/4 cup cream
2 tablespoons sugar + I tablespoon cinnamon mixed together

Rose & Claire
enjoying a
morning muffin.

1. Preheat oven to 400 degrees.
2. Place first seven ingredients, in food processor and pulse until mixture resembles coarse cornmeal with a few slightly larger butter lumps.
3. Place flour mixture in bowl and add milk.
4. Working quickly, blend ingredients together with a rubber spatula into a soft, slightly wet dough. Turn out onto a lightly floured work surface.
5. Form dough into a disk about 8 to 10 inches in diameter. Cut into 8 wedges. Use a 2-inch round cookie cutter to remove the center of the disk. Place wedges 1-1/2 inches apart on a baking sheet lined with parchment. Brush tops with cream and sprinkle generously with cinnamon sugar mixture.
6. Bake about 12 to 15 minutes until scones are light brown.

Makes 8 large or 16 small scones.

NOTES:

DRIED CHERRIES, DRIED CRANBERRIES, ALMONDS, ORANGE ZEST, DRIED BLUEBERRIES ARE ALL GOOD ADDITIONS TO THIS RECIPE EITHER IN PLACE OF THE RAISINS OR ADDED WITH THEM.

I LIKE TO MAKE HEART-SHAPED SCONES FOR TEA PARTIES.

orange walnut muffins

This is a wonderful recipe to do at home. It can be mixed and kept in your refrigerator for several days. Just scoop out batter each day for your muffins, and enjoy them freshly baked. They can become addictive!

4 large oranges
4 eggs
I cup sugar
I cup butter
I/2 cup sour cream
4 cups unbleached flour
4 teaspoons baking powder
I teaspoon baking soda
I/2 teaspoon salt
I/2 cup walnuts, chopped & toasted

1. Preheat oven to 400 degrees. Grease muffin tins.
2. Remove zest from oranges and set aside. Trim off and discard pith and white membrane. Cut oranges into small chunks, saving the juice, zest and orange together — it should be about 2 cups. Set aside.
3. Lightly whisk eggs in a large bowl. Add sugar, butter and sour cream and stir well.
4. Combine flour, baking powder, baking soda, and salt in another bowl and stir to blend. Add orange and flour mixture to the egg mixture and stir until blended. Stir in the walnuts.
5. Fill the muffin tins to two thirds full. Bake for about 12 to 15 minutes or until a wooden toothpick comes out clean when inserted into the center of a muffin.

Makes II or I2 muffins.

WAKE UP AND SMELL THE MUFFINS!

orange butter

We make this butter several times during the week in large batches to serve with our muffins, pancakes and scones. It's so nice to keep in the fridge — easy, too!

1 whole orange, unpeeled
1 pound butter

❶ Cut orange in chunks (discarding seeds and ends only).
❷ Place orange and butter in food processor and blend until smooth.

Makes 2 cups

ORANGE BUTTER, ROSES AND GERANIUM LEAVES

ginger pear muffins

Fresh pears and ginger combine to make these delicious muffins.
Treat yourself to one as soon as they come from the oven!

3 cups flour
1/3 cup granulated sugar
1/3 cup brown sugar
1 tablespoon baking powder
1 teaspoon salt
1/2 teaspoon baking soda
3 eggs
1/2 cup butter, melted
1 cup yogurt or buttermilk
1 cup pear, finely chopped
4 tablespoons fresh ginger, grated

❶ Preheat oven to 400 degrees.
❷ Mix flour, sugars, baking powder, salt and soda in a large bowl.
❸ In a separate bowl, mix eggs, butter, and yogurt.
❹ Fold liquid ingredients into dry, mixing just until moistened.
❺ Stir in pears and ginger.
❻ Spoon batter into greased or lined muffin tins two-thirds full.
❼ Bake for 20 minutes or until a wooden toothpick comes out
clean when inserted into center of muffin.

Makes 12 to 18 muffins.

NOTE:

THE EASIEST WAY I'VE

FOUND TO CHOP GINGER

IS TO PEEL AND PLACE IN

FOOD PROCESSOR. PULSE

UNTIL DESIRED TEXTURE.

VARIATION:

APPLE WALNUT MUFFINS

— OMIT PEARS AND

GINGER, ADD 3/4 OR

1 CUP CHOPPED APPLES,

1/2 CUP TOASTED PECANS

OR WALNUTS, AND 1/2

TEASPOON CINNAMON.

chewy brown sugar muffins

I really enjoy these muffins - they are both hearty and healthy tasting.

1 cup buttermilk
1 cup maple syrup
2 eggs
1/2 cup whole wheat flour
1 cup unbleached flour
1/4 cup dark brown sugar, firmly packed
1 teaspoon salt
2 teaspoons baking powder
1 teaspoon baking soda
1-1/2 cups rolled oats
1 cup walnuts, coarsely chopped

NOTE:

THESE MUFFINS ARE

VERY NICE SERVED

IN THE FALL.

1. Preheat oven to 350 degrees. Grease muffin tins.
2. In large mixing bowl, combine buttermilk, syrup, eggs, flours, brown sugar, salt, baking powder, soda and oats. Beat with whisk (this is so easy that you don't need an electric anything to make these.) Stir in walnuts.
3. Fill muffin tins to two thirds full.
4. Bake about 20 minutes, or until a wooden toothpick comes out clean when inserted in the center.

Makes 12 muffins.

muesli

This recipe is so nice to have in your refrigerator for you and your guests! It keeps well for several days and is nutritious as well as delicious!

3/4 cup quick oats
3/4 cup skim milk
1/2 cup yogurt
1/4 cup golden raisins
1/4 cup dark raisins
1 tablespoon maple syrup
1/4 cup slivered almonds, toasted
1 green apple, chopped

❶ Mix together first six ingredients and let soak overnight or several hours.
❷ Add almonds and apple and mix well to combine.

Makes 2 to 2-1/2 cups.

NOTES:

I PREFER TO BUY THE

NUTS AND SEEDS FOR

THIS RECIPE FROM THE

REFRIGERATOR SECTION

AT THE HEALTH FOOD

STORE, SO THAT I CAN

BE CONFIDENT OF THE

FRESHNESS.

BE CAREFUL TO ADD

THE RAISINS AFTER

BAKING — I LEARNED

THIS THE HARD WAY

YEARS AGO WHEN I

MIXED IN THE RAISINS,

BAKED IT TOGETHER AND

HAD VERY OVERCOOKED

AND TOUGH RAISINS!

granola

This is my new granola with all the goodness but with less oil this time. We like to serve it for breakfast in the Tea Room with plain (unflavored) yogurt and fresh fruit. It's also a good addition to pancake batter — or sprinkled on top when served.

4-1/2 cups rolled oats
1/2 cup walnuts, chopped coarsely
1/2 cup sunflower seeds
1/2 cup almonds
1/2 cup cashew, pieces
1/2 cup pumpkin seeds
3/4 cup maple syrup
1/4 cup honey
1/4 cup canola oil
1 teaspoon vanilla
1-1/2 cups dark raisins

❶ Place rolled oats, walnuts, sunflower seeds, almonds, cashews and pumpkin seeds in bowl and mix well.
❷ Mix together syrup, honey, canola oil and vanilla and pour over dry ingredients, coating thoroughly.
❸ Place in large shallow pan and bake at 350 degrees for 45 to 60 minutes, stirring every 10 minutes until browned.
❹ Add raisins. Allow to cool and refrigerate in airtight container. Keeps in refrigerator for up to two weeks.

Makes 9-1/2 cups.

breakfast tacos

I love to eat tacos in the morning or anytime! It's important to me to heat the tortillas the way Hector's family taught me — on a hot cast iron griddle. Tortillas can also be heated over a flame if you have a gas cook top. Either way, heat the tortilla until it begins to puff and gets a bit of golden color. This brings you much closer to a product that tastes "just made!"

8 eggs
4 tablespoons butter, melted
4 flour tortillas
1 cup Rosemary Garlic Roasted Potatoes (see Side Dishes)
4 tablespoons Tea Room Pico de Gallo (see Appetizer)
6 tablespoons Monterey Jack cheese, shredded

1 Scramble eggs in butter.
2 Divide eggs among the tortillas. Top with potatoes, Peach Tree Pico de Gallo and cheese.
3 Serve immediately.

Makes 4 tacos.

VARIATIONS:

ROASTED TOMATOES, WILTED SPINACH, ROSEMARY, ROASTED POTATOES, BACON, QUESO FRESCO — CHOOSE YOUR COMBINATION — YOU CAN'T MISS!

NOTE:

A FAVORITE BREAKFAST

OF MINE IS A BLUEBERRY

PANCAKE TOPPED WITH

FRESH PEACHES, A SCOOP

OF NONFAT UNFLAVORED

YOGURT AND JUST A

DRIZZLE OF MAPLE

SYRUP — LOTS OF

FLAVOR AND NO NEED

FOR BUTTER! FOR

BLUEBERRY PANCAKES

I LIKE TO SPRINKLE

THE BERRIES ON TOP OF

THE BATTER BEFORE

FLIPPING — OTHER

POSSIBILITIES CAN BE

FRESH STRAWBERRIES,

CHOCOLATE CHIPS,

GRANOLA, PINEAPPLE,

APPLE SLICES, WALNUTS.

multi grain pancakes

Pancakes have always been part of Sunday morning in our house-hold. I have made a few changes since the recipe was published in my first cookbook. This is a good variation and is the one we serve in the Tea Room for breakfast - with heart shaped butter and pure maple syrup.

I cup unbleached flour
I/2 cup whole wheat flour
I/2 cup oats
2 tablespoons white corn meal
I/2 teaspoon soda
I tablespoon sugar
I/2 teaspoon salt
2 teaspoons baking powder
I/2 cup buttermilk
3/4 cup skim milk
2 eggs

❶ Combine all dry ingredients in bowl. Add buttermilk, skim milk and eggs, and stir only until mixed. The batter will be lumpy.

❷ Heat a small amount of oil in skillet or griddle until a drop of water sizzles on it. Pour batter into pan, making pancakes about 3-1/2 inches in diameter. Cook over medium heat until bubbles appear on top. Flip pancakes over and continue cooking until golden. Serve immediately with butter and maple syrup.

Makes 4 servings

jp's french toast

My friend, John Phelps, was managing our Tea Room when we made the decision to serve breakfast. One of his great contributions to our menu is his recipe for this delicious French Toast. The addition of fresh orange zest and Grand Marnier to this recipe makes breakfast a grand and elegant occasion.

6 eggs
1-1/3 cups orange juice
1/3 cup Grand Marnier
1/3 cup whole milk
3 tablespoons sugar
1/4 teaspoon vanilla
1/4 teaspoon salt
Zest of 1 orange
1 loaf French bread, slightly dry, (8 diagonal slices, 3/4-inch thick)
1/4 cup butter to melt in pan

❶ Beat eggs in bowl. Add orange juice, Grand Marnier, milk, sugar, vanilla, salt and orange zest; mix well.
❷ Dip bread slices into egg mixture, turning to coat all surfaces. Transfer to a glass baking dish in a single layer. Pour any remaining egg mixture over the top. Soak bread slices until soggy or overnight if desired.
❸ Melt butter in large skillet over medium-high heat. Add bread slices and cook until golden brown. Turn over once and brown other side.

Makes 4 servings.

peachy french toast

Topping:
8 tablespoons coconut
2-1/2 cups peaches, sliced
1/4 cup brandy
1/2 cup Cream of Coconut

❶ Place coconut in shallow baking pan - toast in oven at 350 degrees until golden, set aside.
❷ Combine peaches, cream of Coconut and brandy in skillet. Cook for 8 to 10 minutes. Serve spooned on french toast (recipe follows).
❸ Sprinkle toasted coconut over peaches.

French toast:
1 loaf French bread, slightly dry, (8 diagonal slices, 3/4 inch thick)
6 eggs
1 cup milk
1 tablespoon vanilla
1 teaspoon cinnamon
1 teaspoon nutmeg

❶ Combine milk, eggs and vanilla in shallow bowl. Soak bread slices in milk mixture until soggy.
❷ Heat 1/4 inch oil in skillet. Fry toast until golden on both sides. Sprinkle with powdered sugar. Serve with maple syrup and fresh fruit.

Makes 4 servings

PEACHY FRENCH TOAST

evelyn's peach preserves

Evelyn makes preserves every week so our breakfast customers can enjoy the fresh taste of this Fredericksburg treat! The microwave does the work while Evelyn makes the delicious cheesecakes that we serve in our Tea Room.

4 cups peaches, peeled and chopped
1 package "no sugar" fruit pectin
1 cup water
3 cups sugar
2 tablespoons lemon juice

❶ Place peaches, pectin and water in 8 cup or larger microwave container or glass measuring cup. (If peaches are juicy - do not add water). Microwave for 10 minutes on High. Use caution in handling the microwaved preserves as they are boiling hot.
❷ Add sugar and lemon juice and microwave 10 more minutes.
❸ Let the preserves cool before refrigerating.
❹ Refrigerate until used.

Makes 6 cups.

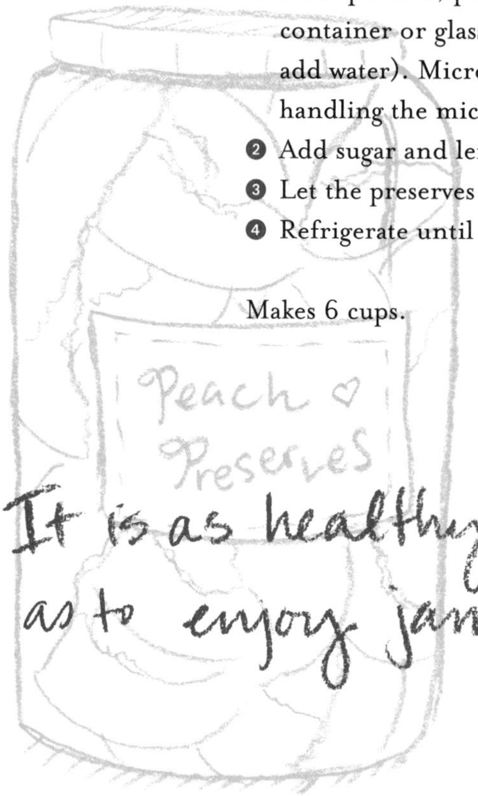

It is as healthy to enjoy sentiment as to enjoy jam.

G.K. Chesterson

24

yogurt cheese

I like to use this spread in place of cream cheese for veggie sandwiches. There are many ways to enjoy it —mix in strawberry jam for muffins —or mix in fresh garlic and herbs for a delicious and guilt-free party spread!

2 cups low fat plain yogurt

❶ Place yogurt in a colander that is lined with cheesecloth. Set over a bowl, cover with a damp cloth or plastic wrap and place in refrigerator to drain for several hours or overnight.

❷ Remove from refrigerator and place the drained yogurt in a small bowl, cover and place in refrigerator until ready to use. Discard the drained liquid.

Makes almost 2 cups.

hill country eggs benedict

2 slices Jalapeño Cheese Bread, toasted (See Breads)
2 slices bacon, fried
2 poached eggs
1/4 cup Hollandaise Sauce (recipe to follow on next page)

Place 2 slices toasted bread on warmed plate, top with bacon slices, eggs and pour Hollandaise Sauce over top.

Makes 1 serving.

Tina's Tip

Tina and I were called into the Tea Room for early breakfast duty when our chef went on vacation for a week. I did the morning baking and Tina was in charge of the grill. Our chef had shown her how to make our Hollandaise Sauce for the Hill Country Eggs Benedict — one of our most popular breakfast dishes.

It took her 45 minutes to make the sauce, and thinking there had to be an easier way, she called our friend, Sean Wilkinson, owner and chef of The Nest Restaurant. Sean graciously talked her through the recipe and she was then able to make the Hollandaise Sauce in five to ten minutes!

Tina and I had a good laugh and decided that our chef had sent her on a kitchen version of a snipe hunt while he was enjoying his vacation.

Tina's advice in making this sauce is to have all of your ingredients ready before you begin. It takes some practice, but when mastered, you, like Tina, can be very proud of your accomplishment.

hollandaise sauce

Juice of 1 lemon (about 2 tablespoons)
1 teaspoon garlic, minced
2 tablespoons white wine
6 egg yolks
2 cups butter, melted
1 teaspoon cayenne pepper
1 teaspoon Kosher salt

NOTE:

YOU'LL KNOW IT'S RIGHT

WHEN YOU TASTE THE

SAUCE AND THE CAYENNE

PEPPER TICKLES THE

BACK OF YOUR THROAT.

❶ In a double boiler, whisk the lemon juice, garlic, wine and egg yolks over low heat. Whisk briskly for about 5 minutes until the mixture thickens, being careful to scrape the sides of the pan as you whisk.

❷ Remove from heat and place pan immediately onto a towel that has been soaked under cold running water. Whisk briskly as you slowly pour the melted butter into the sauce. This is a tricky step – the best way to do this is to pour slowly about one third of the butter, continuously whisking even as you pour. The sauce will become thicker as the butter is added.

❸ Add cayenne pepper and salt to taste.

Makes 2-1/2 cups.

Thoughts

My cosmos was planted in front of the Peach Tree 15 years ago from half a cup of seed given to me by Carol Bade from her garden. Thousands of tiny plants faithfully burst into view every spring, then they reseed themselves several times during the growing season, until the frost puts them to sleep for the winter months. And then it springs to new life again — Spring bursting forth from the death of winter.

"His mercies are new every morning - great is His faithfulness."

The principle of death and resurrection is everywhere — clean air after a thunderstorm — flowers and baby green leaves after the bare branches of winter — laughter after tears — delicious crusty bread from dying yeast — new life is all around us — over and over again we experience and believe resurrection life when we lose someone so dear to our hearts in death.

LYDIA CUTTING COSMOS

28

appetizers

crostini topper ideas:

GOAT CHEESE SPREAD topped with Sun Dried Tomato Pesto.

BLUE CHEESE, a thin slice of pear, and finely chopped walnuts.

CREAM CHEESE with a little bit of horseradish and lemon mixed in, thin slice of smoked salmon topped with finely chopped red onion, or capers, or BOTH! A dill sprig is a fresh pretty touch.

SLICE OF FRESH MOZZARELLA, whole sage leaf, and a light sprinkle of fresh grated Parmesan - bake at 400 degrees until cheese is melted, serve at once.

FRESH GUACAMOLE with a light sprinkle of grated Cotija cheese.

CREAM CHEESE or goat cheese, topped with a little cherry tomato flower filled with Artichoke Pesto (this section).

TOMATOES, chopped small, thin slices of garlic, fresh basil, all tossed together with a drizzle of olive oil.

ROASTED EGGPLANT, ZUCCHINI AND RED PEPPERS, chopped and tossed together. Garnish with a tiny sprig of thyme or a yellow flower petal, such as cosmos.

peach tree crostini

Crostini has become one of my favorite appetizers. It is the perfect "gathering" food. The bread slices are toasted early in the day and the toppings are spooned on top and garnished just as the first guests are arriving. They are so pretty when placed on trays and passed around to your guests.

I sometimes pile the Crostini slices in a basket, surrounded by little bowls filled with toppings and everyone "designs" his own Crostini creation.

1 loaf Peach Tree Country French Bread (see Breads), or good quality home style loaf of bread, cut into 1/4 inch thick slices
Olive oil

1. Preheat oven to 400 degrees.
2. Brush slices of French Bread lightly with olive oil.
3. Place in single layer, on baking sheet. Place in oven until toasted golden brown — for 8 to 10 minutes.

NOTE:

THE NUMBER OF SLICES WILL VARY ACCORDING TO THE BREAD YOU USE — WHEN WE MAKE CROSTINI IN THE TEA ROOM WE FORM OUR LOAVES LONG AND NARROW AND CAN GET 50-60 SLICES.

gathering Food!

Basil - symbol of love and devotion —

sun-dried tomato pesto

NOTE:

IT'S ALSO GOOD SPREAD

UNDER THE SKIN OF

CHICKEN WHEN GRILLING

OR BAKING — AND I

SERVE IT OFTEN WITH

GOAT CHEESE SPREAD ON

PEACH TREE CROSTINI

(THIS SECTION) AS AN

APPETIZER.

This recipe is in our second book, **The Peach Tree Family Cookbook**, and I wanted to include it here so you can make the Sun-Dried Tomato Pesto Bread (see Breads).

1/2 cup sun-dried tomatoes, softened in hot water, and drained
3/4 cup walnuts, toasted
1 cup fresh basil
3/4 cup olive oil
3/4 cup Parmesan cheese, grated
6 garlic cloves
1 teaspoon pepper, freshly ground
Salt to taste

Measure all ingredients into food processor. Process until ingredients are thoroughly chopped. Taste for salt. Refrigerate.

Makes 1-1/2 cups.

artichoke pesto

NOTE:

BEST IF MADE SEVERAL

HOURS OR A DAY AHEAD

SO THE FLAVORS CAN

INTENSIFY!

Delicious spread on slices of crusty bread or crackers — and of course as a topping for Peach Tree Crostini (see Appetizers).

1 can artichoke hearts
3 tablespoons lemon juice (juice of 1 lemon)
1/4 cup olive oil
6 to 10 cloves Roasted Garlic (see Side Dishes)
1/4 teaspoon salt

Put all ingredients in food processor and chop finely.

Makes 1-3/4 cups.

crostini toppers

Party Food!

I treasure my friendship with John Phelps. His family moved to Fredericksburg at the time we opened the Tea Room — his dad was David's and Carlos' Scout leader. JP would come by and visit me when he was home from school. Later he worked for us managing our Tea Room — I have enjoyed our "food talks" for what seems like forever — he shares my passion for enjoying good food, and using his entertaining talents to bring friends together around the table. This is one of his "best of the best" recipes. He likes this recipe for entertaining because he can mix it early in the day — then bake it just before party time and keep it warm in his oven until time to serve.

hot spinach dipping sauce with chipotle cream

2 chipotle chiles, canned with Adobo Sauce
1 cup half and half, divided use
2 fresh serrano chile peppers, seeded and chopped
2 jalapeños, seeded and chopped
1 small onion, chopped
2 tablespoons vegetable oil
2 fresh tomatoes, peeled, seeded and chopped
1 10-ounce package frozen chopped spinach,
thawed and squeezed dry
1 tablespoon red wine vinegar
8 ounces cream cheese, room temperature
2 cups Monterey Jack cheese, grated
Salt and pepper, freshly ground, to taste

❶ Preheat oven to 400 degrees.
❷ Pureé chipotle chiles with 2 tablespoons of half and half.
   Set aside.
❸ In a small skillet, cook the serrano chiles and jalapeños with the
   onion in oil over moderate heat. Stir for 4 to 6 minutes, or until
   onion is softened.
❹ Add tomatoes, and heat the mixture, stirring for 2 minutes.
❺ Transfer the mixture to a bowl and stir in spinach, vinegar, cream
   cheese, Monterey Jack cheese and remaining half and half. Add
   salt and pepper to taste.
❻ Transfer dipping sauce to a buttered 10-inch round baking dish
   and bake for 30 to 40 minutes, or until it is hot and bubbly.
❼ Drizzle chipotle-cream mixture over the dip. Serve with tortilla
   chips or Peach Tree Crostini (see this section).

Makes 10 servings.

♥ **NOTE:**

CAN BE STORED IN AIR

TIGHT CONTAINER FOR 8

TO 10 DAYS.

pepitas
(roasted spiced pumpkin seeds)

As a child I loved to snack on "pepitas." As an adult I find they are delicious served as an appetizer with margaritas or beer. They are a tasty accent to sprinkle on salads or on top of Sweet Potato Jalapeño Soup (see Soups) — also an important ingredient for the Texana Bread (see Breads) that we serve in the Tea Room.

1 tablespoon garlic powder
1 tablespoon chile powder
2 to 3 tablespoons olive oil
2 cups pumpkin seeds

❶ Preheat oven to 350 degrees.
❷ Mix all ingredients.
❸ Spread on cookie sheet. Bake for 20 to 25 minutes.

Makes 2 cups.

A good meal ought to begin with

maple chile pecans

NOTE:

IF YOU LIKE A LITTLE

MORE SPICE ADD A DASH

OF CAYENNE PEPPER.

I love to sprinkle these on salads — especially in fall and winter with pears or apples and bleu cheese — and they make very good nibbling!!

2 cups pecans (or walnuts)
4 tablespoons maple syrup
2 tablespoons chile powder

❶ Place pecans and maple syrup in mixing bowl. Toss to coat well.
❷ Place on baking sheet and bake for 15 to 20 minutes at 350 degrees until toasted a golden color.
❸ Remove from oven and sprinkle with chile powder. Cool completely. Store in tightly sealed container.

Makes 2 cups.

hunger
French Proverb

What a beautiful sight! A collection of sun blessed tomatoes on my table!

tea room pico de gallo

Simple ingredients — such an important addition to our breakfast tacos. It is wonderful to have in your fridge to dress up omelets, chalupas, baked potatoes, or freshly fried tortilla chips when entertaining in the summertime, or anytime! Very often Hector and I will enjoy a bowl of pinto beans and brown rice for dinner. It's good for us and when topped with a spoonful of this pico de gallo we are most supremely happy!

8 tomatoes, coarsely chopped
4 fresh jalapeños, finely chopped
1-1/2 cups white onion, finely chopped
Juice of one lime
1 cup cilantro, coarsely chopped
1 teaspoon salt

Hand chop all ingredients. Mix together. Keeps in refrigerator for 4 to 5 days.

Makes about 6 cups.

NOTE:

THIS CAN BE DONE IN THE FOOD PROCESSOR IF YOU PREFER, BUT I, MYSELF, LIKE IT HAND CHOPPED THE WAY WE DO IT IN THE TEA ROOM KITCHEN FOR A NICER APPEARANCE. IT'S A PREFERENCE THING!!

gorditas

Hector's sister, Teresita, gave me this recipe. She and her family own a Mexican restaurant in Northern California. These fat little tortillas are delicious appetizers when topped with refried beans, shredded lettuce, grated cheese and fresh Tea Room Pico de Gallo. Or if you eat several - it's dinner!

3 cups Masa Harina
1 cup unbleached flour
4 teaspoons baking powder
1 teaspoon salt
3 tablespoons shortening
1-1/2 cups hot water
Canola oil for frying - 1/2 inch to 1 inch oil in skillet

Toppings:
Refried beans
Lettuce, sliced very thinly
Fresh Tea Room Pico de Gallo (see this section)
Grated cheese (Cheddar or Monterey Jack - I love to use freshly grated Cotija if available)

❶ Thoroughly mix all ingredients, except water and canola oil.
❷ Add very hot water (from the tap) to make a soft workable dough. If necessary, add more water a tablespoon at a time.
❸ Cover dough with damp cloth. Allow dough to rest for 20 to 30 minutes.
❹ By hand, form into 3-inch patties about 1/2 inch thick and fry in hot oil. Place on paper towels to drain excess oil.
❺ Serve immediately with any or all of the toppings suggested.

Makes 10.

black bean-corn salsa

As a toddler, Andrew Cox visited The Peach Tree Gift Shop with
his mother long before we were even thinking of opening the Tea
Room. I've watched him grow up and now that he has his own
home it's such fun to have him share his recipe with me. He says of
this recipe that it's "enough to feed Cox's Army!!"

3 cans black beans, rinsed and drained
1 can yellow corn, drained
2 cans white shoe peg corn, drained
1 red bell pepper, chopped
1 green or yellow pepper, chopped
1 red onion, chopped
3 cans Rotel tomatoes, partially drained
3 fresh jalapeños, finely chopped - include seeds of 1 jalapeño
1 cup cilantro, coarsely chopped
1/4 cup red wine vinegar
Juice of 1 lemon
2 garlic cloves, minced
1 teaspoon chile powder
1 teaspoon comino
1 teaspoon salt

- cilantro

Mix all ingredients together. Chill well and serve with tostadas.

Makes 2 quarts.

N O T E :

REMEMBER YOU CAN

ALWAYS PROCESS (CHOP)

IT AGAIN WHEN RECIPE IS

COMPLETED IF YOU

DESIRE A FINER TEXTURE.

cranberry salsa

I buy cranberries the moment I see them in the market just so I can make this salsa. It's a great appetizer to serve next to a bowl of tortilla chips for dipping — and as a topping for cream cheese or goat cheese spread on Peach Tree Crostini (see this section).

3 oranges, cut in quarters, seeds removed
2 jalapeños, seeded
2 cups sugar, divided use
1 bunch cilantro
8 cups cranberries

❶ Chop oranges, jalapeños and 1/2 cup sugar in food processor, being careful not to chop too finely - some texture is nice in this recipe. Put in mixing bowl.
❷ Chop cilantro and half of cranberries and add 1/2 cup sugar. Combine with first mixture.
❸ Chop rest of cranberries with 1 cup sugar and add to mix.

Makes 6 to 8 cups.

Colorful and tasty holiday food!

marinated shrimp and jalapeños

This is such an easy and versatile way to prepare shrimp! All the ingredients are tossed together and baked right in the serving dish. It's good served right from the oven over pasta or cooled to room temperature and served with fresh fried tortilla chips for appetizing — or placed in the refrigerator until well chilled and served on top of crispy bean and cheese chalupas!

2 tablespoons olive oil
2 pounds shrimp, shelled and deveined (20 to 24 per pound)
1 large onion, sliced
3 tablespoons canned jalapeños, cut into thin strips
1/2 cup cilantro leaves, chopped
Salt to taste
Juice of 1 lime

1 Preheat oven to 400 degrees.
2 Mix together all ingredients except lime juice - place in
   9 x 13-inch baking dish. Bake for 20 minutes.
3 Remove from oven and squeeze fresh lime juice over it.
4 Serve hot or cold with lime wedges or lime slices and a bowl
   of fresh tortilla chips.

Makes 12 to 15 appetizer servings.

Carlos' Catch

Hector, Tina and I have such sweet memories of our time spent with Carlos at the 4UR Ranch in Creede, Colorado. Fly fishing was one of his great loves and usually he would catch and release, but not always. The cook at the ranch was always willing to prepare the trout he caught for his meal. One time Carlos asked to have his trout prepared with this recipe so we could all share. It was such a lovely evening — sharing his "catch," sipping wine, enjoying the mountain air and big sky... and each other.

trout mousse

2 quarts water
I rib celery, finely chopped
I/2 bunch green onions, finely chopped
I/2 tablespoon whole black peppercorns
I/2 cup lemon juice, divided use
3 (10 inch) fresh trout, heads and tails removed
2 8-ounce packages cream cheese, softened
2 tablespoons lemon juice
I teaspoon liquid smoke
I/4 teaspoon salt
I/4 teaspoon pepper
I tablespoon fresh chopped dill
I tablespoon fresh chopped chives
2 cloves garlic, finely chopped
I tablespoon finely chopped red onion

❶ Bring water, celery, green onions, peppercorns and I/4 cup
  lemon juice to a simmer.
❷ Add fish and simmer for I5 minutes. Remove fish and discard
  stock. Cool for 30 minutes.
❸ Meanwhile, with a mixer, whip cream cheese until light and
  fluffy, about 5 minutes. Add the rest of the ingredients (except
  fish) and whip for another two minutes.
❹ Scrape down sides of bowl and mix I more minute. Make sure
  there are no lumps. If not smooth, mix again.
❺ Remove the fish flesh from the bones and add to cream cheese
  mixture. Mix on medium speed for I minute. Taste and adjust
  seasonings, if necessary, with salt and pepper.
❻ Refrigerate, covered, until needed. Keeps in the refrigerator
  for up to I week. Serve with crackers or Peach Tree Crostini
  (see this section).

Makes I2 servings.

carpaccio

In Fredericksburg, every two years, the Friends of the Hospital sponsor a Gala for the purpose of raising money to make our outstanding facility even better. There is a group of us who were supper club members 15 years ago — we offer "Dinner for 12" as a silent auction item. We come together to plan and then to prepare a special meal for the highest bidder. It is a very special time of reunion for all of us who for many years have shared our love of entertaining. We have great memories of learning together as we've been challenged to try new dishes. A wonderful time is had by all. This is Susan Rees' recipe for Carpaccio — I love when it's on our menu. We always prepare extra of everything so the cooks can eat, too!

I pound beef tenderloin, trimmed of all fat and sinew
4 cups arugula, leaves chopped
I/4 cup capers
I/3 cup Parmesan cheese shavings
I/4 to I/2 cup extra-virgin olive oil
Black pepper to taste, freshly ground
Garnish: lemon wedges

❶ Freeze the tenderloin and then allow to thaw slightly in the refrigerator (about 4 hours). Slice the beef into paper-thin slices. An electric slicer does the best job.

❷ Arrange the beef slices on a serving plate and top with arugula, capers, and Parmesan shavings.

❸ Drizzle with olive oil and liberally dust with pepper to taste. Garnish with lemon wedges and serve with a good crusty French or Italian bread.

NOTE:

THE MOST IMPORTANT THING TO MAKE THIS RECIPE SUCCESSFUL IS EXTREMELY HIGH QUALITY BEEF. IT IS IMPORTANT FOR ME TO MENTION HERE THAT YOU MUST BE VERY CAREFUL TO KNOW THE SOURCE OF THE BEEF YOU WILL BE USING BECAUSE OF THE RECENT PUBLICITY CONCERNING CONTAMINATION OF MEATS.

drinks

I serve Sangria in the summertime —
It looks inviting in a tall pitcher with
citrus slices floating. An easy drink
to serve when entertaining friends at home

SANGRIA

sangria

GARNISH:

ORANGE, LEMON AND

LIME SLICES

6 cups Burgundy table wine
1 cup Citrus Syrup (see this Section)
1 small can frozen limeade concentrate

Mix together all ingredients. Serve over ice.

Makes 8 cups.

sangria blanca

GARNISH:

GREEN GRAPES, LIME

AND ORANGE SLICES.

Very light and pretty version of Sangria — sparkling water can be a refreshing addition.

6 cups Chablis table wine
1 cup Citrus Syrup (see this Section)
1 small can frozen limeade concentrate

Mix together all ingredients. Serve over ice.

Makes 8 cups.

citrus syrup

I use this syrup to add flavor to my Sangria (see this section) and it's nice to keep in the refrigerator for making quick delicious drinks in the summertime, too.

2 cups water
2 cups sugar
1 orange, 1 lemon, 1 lime, cut in slices

Bring all to a boil - cook gently for 20 to 30 minutes. Let rest for 1/2 hour - strain and discard fruit. Use syrup immediately or refrigerate until needed.

Makes 3 cups.

citrus - chablis cooler

Pour a little Citrus Syrup and white wine over ice — and top it off with a splash of sparkling water.

lemon - a symbol of fidelity

altar society punch

My Aunt Mella was known as the "Punch Queen" when she attended Our Lady of Grace Church in San Antonio. I've served this delicious recipe at wedding receptions and I always receive compliments and requests for the recipe.

I can (46 ounce) apricot nectar
I can (46 ounce) pineapple juice
3 cans (6 ounce) frozen limeade
3 quarts ginger ale, chilled

❶ Mix all ingredients except ginger ale together and chill.
❷ Immediately before serving, add the 3 quarts chilled ginger ale.

Makes approximately 50 cups.

NOTES:

THIS PUNCH IS REALLY GOOD JUST AS WRITTEN, BUT IF YOU WANT TO LIVEN IT UP YOU CAN ADD VODKA, GIN OR RUM.

I LIKE TO SERVE THIS PUNCH IN A TALL HAND BLOWN GLASS CYLINDER GARNISHED WITH FRESH FLOWERS AND LIME SLICES. SOMETIMES I MAKE A FROZEN ICE MOLD TO FLOAT — IT'S PRETTY AND KEEPS THE PUNCH CHILLED.

IF DESIRED, PREPARE A RING MOLD OF FROZEN GINGER ALE TO HELP KEEP PUNCH COLD AND UNDILUTED.

fruit smoothie

This drink combines some of my favorite flavors - becoming a complete breakfast. Add protein powder or brewer's yeast if you like — or bran for extra fiber.

3 tablespoons Créme de Coconut
1 small banana
4 to 5 medium sized strawberries
1 orange, seeded, peeled and quartered
1/2 cup skim milk
1 cup ice

Place all ingredients in blender and blend until smooth.

Makes 2 servings.

hot toddy

My Aunt Mella brought me this recipe when I was suffering from a frustrating sinus condition — with the following note. "If this doesn't open your sinuses - try dynamite!" It's nice to have a recipe for this good old fashioned remedy. You just never know when it may come in handy for a cure!

1 cup hot tea
Lemon and honey to taste
1 or 2 jiggers of your favorite libation - bourbon, scotch, brandy, etc.

Mix all the above. Sip slowly while piping hot.

Makes 1 serving.

ginger lemonade

3 to 4 tablespoons Citrus Syrup with Ginger
3 to 4 tablespoons lemon juice

❶ Add a 1 to 2-inch piece of fresh ginger to above Citrus Syrup when making the syrup.
❷ Pour syrup and fresh lemon juice in a glass of ice. Pour water or sparkling water to fill the glass. Garnish. Sit down in your garden, rest and enjoy!

house tea recipe

Here is the recipe for the delicious lemon orange tea that we have served in our Tea Room since we opened in 1983. It continues to be my personal favorite. The flavor is gentle, light and refreshing — a Peach Tree classic.

3 bags Lipton Orange Garden (decaf)
1 bag Bigelow Lemon Lift
1 quart boiling water

❶ Pour boiling water over tea bags.
❷ Steep 5 to 10 minutes. Remove teabags.
❸ Add 1 quart room temperature water. Stir and serve over ice.

Makes 1/2 gallon.

mint- a symbol of virtue.

soups

ONE OF THE LITTLE MIRACLES THAT WE ALL SO enjoy at the table is the delightful experience which happens when we are served something attractively. And to me, soups and salads, because of the fresh ingredients used, can be the most fun to embellish.

The easiest way for me to decide about garnishing food is to consider the color, texture and taste of the dish I'm wanting to decorate. For instance, the **Pinto Bean Soup** is a very simple soup, but when the Tea Room Pico de Gallo is placed on top, it sparkles in appearance and in flavor. The **Chicken and Noodle Dumplings** is beautiful and exciting visually with the heart shaped noodles floating amongst the carrots, and if anything at all is needed, it might be a simple sprinkling of finely chopped parsley leaves, but it could easily stand alone.

When you are deciding how to garnish a dish, it's good to consider the ingredients that are being used in a dish. For example, a salad such as the **Holiday Chicken Salad** has walnuts mixed into the ingredients, so a sprinkling of chopped toasted walnuts is an obvious choice.

Sometimes it's just the mixture of the ingredients that makes the dish look attractive, as in the **French Lentil Salad** recipe. The red onions and red peppers both add a nice tasty crunchy texture, and when the red peppers are chopped or sliced into long slivers, the salad really needs nothing more — the garnish is the dish itself.

We cooks have special opportunities to create "a thing of beauty" every time we prepare a meal or even just a snack. If it's a challenge to you now, just begin - practice and have some fun in the process. The possibilities are endless - just think, there are new ways of putting it all together for all of us to discover!

soup & salad garnishes

PEPITAS: Chile Roasted Spiced Pumpkin Seeds - Pepitas (see Appetizers).

TOASTED SUNFLOWER SEEDS: Raw sunflower seeds, toss lightly with olive oil and toast in a moderate oven until light brown. Toss with a small bit of Kosher salt.

FRIED TORTILLA NOODLES: Corn tortillas, cut into thin strips and fried until crispy.

FRIED PARSLEY SPRIGS: Dip parsley stems into hot oil for a few seconds, drain on paper towels — they get crispy as they cool.

TINY CROUTONS: Trim crusts from slices of white bread - roll slices out thin and cut into 1/4 inch pieces - saute in a little butter and olive oil until golden.

FLOWER CONFETTI: Gather flowers from your garden and carefully remove the petals. With a very sharp cook's knife chop the petals into tiny confetti bits. Use immediately or place in a covered container and keep refrigerated for one or two days.

BASIL CONFETTI: Layer basil leaves, 6 to 10 together - hold securely in one hand and slice very thin strips with a sharp knife or scissors.

ROASTED GARLIC CRÉME FRÂICHE: 1 cup Créme Frâiche and 1 tablespoon Roasted Garlic. Place in food processor and mix until very smooth - it will become runny but will thicken after about an hour of refrigeration. Good garnish for soups.

ROASTED RED PEPPER CRÉME FRÂICHE: 1 cup Créme Frâiche (see Desserts) and 2 tablespoons Roasted Red Peppers (see Side Dishes). Place in blender and mix until smooth - it will become runny but will thicken after an hour of refrigeration. (Use a blender for this rather than a food processor so that the color of the pepper is released throughout the Créme Frâiche.) Good and flavorful garnish for soups.

FRESH HERB SPRIGS: Such as thyme, oregano, basil, rosemary.

SOUR CREAM OR CRÉME FRÂICHE: Fill a squeeze bottle with sour cream, or Créme Frâiche. "Draw" designs on top of chilled soups, or creamy hot soups - we do hearts in the Tea Room — be creative — do initials or flowers! Use every opportunity you can to show others how you care for them.

BRUSCHETTA: Small slices of toasted French bread with creamy mozzarella melted on top and a sprinkle of fresh Parmesan cheese. Delicious floating on top of soup or served as an open faced sandwich.

I PREFER THE CHERRIES

LEFT WHOLE BECAUSE

I LIKE THE TEXTURE.

BUT PUREED IS ALSO

VERY NICE.

THIS IS A GOOD PLACE TO

USE FLOWER CONFETTI

(SEE THIS SECTION) AS

A GARNISH — YELLOW

AND DIFFERENT SHADES

OF PINK WOULD BE

LOVELY.

chilled cherry soup

This soup became part of my recipe collection years ago when Carla Jo Hopkins, who worked in our gift shop, shared it with me. It's as lovely as it is delicious. Serve it for breakfast with muffins — for lunch with quiche or little sandwiches — or dessert with sugar cookies. Anytime!!

1 cup sugar
1 cinnamon stick
3 cups cold water
2 16-ounce cans tart cherries, pitted
1 tablespoon cornstarch
1/2 cup heavy cream
3/4 cup dry red wine
1/2 cup sour cream

❶ In a 2-quart saucepan, combine sugar, cinnamon stick and water. Bring to a boil and add cherries. Partially cover and simmer over low heat for 10 minutes.

❷ Remove cinnamon stick. Add enough of hot liquid to cornstarch to make a paste.

❸ Blend paste into hot cherry mixture. Stir over medium high heat until boiling. Reduce heat and simmer about 2 minutes until clear and thick. Refrigerate until chilled.

❹ To serve, add heavy cream, wine and sour cream. Stir until smooth (leaving cherries whole; or if desired puree in blender until smooth).

Makes 4 cups or 6 servings.

cream of artichoke soup

GARNISH:

HARD COOKED EGG

SLICES, MINCED PARSLEY

OR CHIVES, SOUR CREAM,

LEMON OR LIME SLICE

This is a simple and fast recipe with great artichoke flavor. It came to me from Charles Schmidt via close friends in Mansfield, Texas. Whenever the Schmidts visit the Franks - they are treated to a wonderful meal served on their collection of beautiful antique dishes. A wonderful idea to make special times together even more special!

1 10-ounce can artichokes, water-packed
1-1/4 cups chicken stock
1 teaspoon salt
1/4 teaspoon powdered oregano
2 tablespoons lemon juice
1 cup half and half

❶ Drain artichoke hearts and puree in a blender with chicken stock, salt, oregano and lemon juice. Transfer to saucepan and heat slowly. Cool.

❷ Add half and half and mix well. Chill thoroughly and serve in chilled bowls with garnish.

Makes 4 cups.

cold plum soup

We've used this recipe with great success at our Hospital Gala dinner. Jane Woelhoff's Cold Plum Soup is one that has repeatedly been enjoyed by our guests—and by us, "back stage" in the kitchen. It's beautiful, elegant, and delicious!

1 can purple plums (1 pound 13-ounce) pitted, chopped and liquid reserved
1 cup water
2/3 cup sugar
1 cinnamon stick
1/2 teaspoon white pepper
Salt to taste
1/2 cup heavy cream
1/2 cup dry red wine
1 tablespoon cornstarch
2 tablespoons fresh lemon juice
1 teaspoon lemon zest
1 cup sour cream
3 tablespoons brandy

❶ In saucepan combine plums with reserved liquid, water, sugar, cinnamon stick, white pepper and salt. Bring to boil over moderately high heat.

❷ Reduce heat and cook the mixture, stirring occasionally for 5 minutes. Stir in cream and wine mixed with cornstarch and cook the mixture, stirring until thickened.

❸ Stir in lemon juice and lemon zest. Remove pan from heat.

❹ In a small bowl whisk sour cream into soup mixture with brandy, and stir the soup until it is smooth.

❺ Let the soup cool and chill, covered for at least 4 hours. Ladle in cups and garnish each with a dollop of sour cream and sprinkle with cinnamon and lemon zest.

Makes 6 to 8 servings.

Plums

oma koock's mushroom soup

In our early Fredericksburg days, there was a restaurant called Oma Koock's, owned and operated by Guiche Koock. It was a gathering place — we went often with our young family and always enjoyed seeing our friends. It was a treat to be seated in front of the big fireplace in the wintertime. I don't think of Oma Koock's without this soup as part of the memory. It's one of the best soups — I don't even remember how I got the recipe, but I am so glad I did.

1 pound mushrooms, sliced
1 bunch green onions, finely chopped
2 tablespoons butter
Salt and black pepper, freshly ground, to taste
2 cans beef broth
1 cup water
1/2 cup dry white wine
1 cup whipping cream
2 egg yolks

❶ Saute mushrooms and onions in butter until tender. Season with salt and pepper to taste.
❷ Add broth, water and wine. Cover and simmer 1 hour.
❸ Combine cream with egg yolks. Add some hot soup to cream-egg mixture, a little at a time. Stir heated mixture back into the pot. Bring to serving temperature being careful not to boil as this would curdle the egg yolks.

Makes 6 servings.

My Great Grandmother
Collins' Tureen

NOTES:

To make Summer
Tomato Bisque soup,
remove dill and add
fresh basil for a great
summer variation!

Tomatoes are getting
good press lately for
their health benefits
— another good
reason to enjoy this
soup!

GARNISH:

Roasted Garlic Créme
Frâiche (see Garnishes)
and fresh dill

springtime tomato bisque with fresh dill

The early springtime appearance of dill in my garden led me to develop this recipe. I love the flavor that dill takes on when it is lightly sauteed with garlic and olive oil. It's a delightful tomato soup with intense flavor highlights. When summer arrives, the fresh Basil version is simply wonderful (see Notes).

1 leek, (1-1/2 to 2 cups) sliced 1 inch
4 cloves garlic, sliced in half lengthwise
2 tablespoons butter
2 tablespoons olive oil
1/2 to 1 cup dill
2 28-ounce cans tomatoes
1 14-1/2-ounce can chicken broth
2 teaspoons salt
1/2 teaspoon black pepper, freshly ground
1-1/2 teaspoons sugar
2 cups milk
1/4 teaspoon baking soda

1. Saute leek and garlic in butter and olive oil, until tender.
2. Add dill and saute for 1 minute.
3. Add tomatoes, chicken broth, salt and pepper. Bring to boil, reduce heat and cook for 10 minutes.
4. Remove from heat, let cool for 10 minutes. Puree until smooth.
5. Add sugar, milk and baking soda. Return to heat. Check for seasoning — add salt and pepper if necessary.
6. Garnish and serve.

Makes 8 to 10 cups.

dill

roasted red pepper and garlic soup

Another delicious way to enjoy Roasted Red Peppers and Garlic (see Side Dishes). This soup is thickened by the addition of bread to the broth — a very colorful soup!

3/4 cup garlic cloves, left whole
2 to 3 tablespoons olive oil
2 tablespoons butter, melted
2 onions, sliced
4 to 6 red bell peppers, roasted & peeled (see Sides Dishes)
8 cups chicken broth, divided use
1-1/2 cups day-old French bread, torn into small pieces
1 cup evaporated milk or half and half
Salt and pepper to taste

❶ Place garlic cloves, olive oil and butter in stock pot. Cook slowly over medium heat until the garlic is golden and very tender. Do this slowly… be patient, do not burn the garlic.

❷ Add onions and cover pot, stirring occasionally until the onions are very tender.

❸ Add peppers and 6 cups chicken broth, bring to boil. Simmer for about 15 minutes.

❹ Stir in bread pieces and simmer for 10 minutes, or until bread is very soft.

❺ Puree in blender in small batches, carefully, so that the hot liquid doesn't splash out of container. Use wet towel over the top of jar for protection.

❻ Place soup back into stock pot, add the evaporated milk and remaining chicken stock, and salt and pepper if desired.

Serves 8 to 10.

NOTE:

THESE ARE TWO OF MY

FAVORITE INGREDIENTS,

SO OF COURSE, THEY

INSPIRED ME TO CREATE

A SOUP THAT HAS

BECOME ONE OF OUR

FAMILY'S FAVORITES.

GARNISH:

SWIRL OF CRÉME

FRÂICHE (SEE DESSERTS)

NOTE:

INSTEAD OF DUMPLINGS

USE A 9-OUNCE PACKAGE

OF FRESH FETTUCCINI

NOODLES - CUT INTO

2-INCH LENGTHS AND

YOU HAVE GOOD OLD

FASHIONED CHICKEN

NOODLE SOUP.

chicken and noodle dumplings

One day when Peggy Cox and I were testing recipes in my kitchen, I mentioned I had this wild idea of doing heart shaped noodles to float in the chicken soup. Lo and behold! The next day Peggy brought her mother's noodle dumpling recipe, and we made perfect heart shaped dumplings. We love the way they look when we serve them. Pure and simple…love food!

Soup:
1 4 to 5-pound chicken, cooked, boned
5 quarts water
2 tablespoons salt
1 cup onion, chopped
1 cup celery, sliced
1 cup carrots, sliced

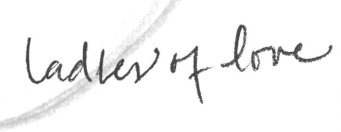

ladles of love

66

1. Place chicken in salted water. Bring to a boil and simmer, covered, for 1-1/2 to 2 hours until tender.
2. Remove from broth, cool slightly. Remove meat from bones, and cut chicken into strips.
3. Measure broth and add enough water if necessary to make 4 quarts liquid. Add onions, celery and carrots and bring to a boil. Reduce heat and cook for 15 to 20 minutes until vegetables are tender. Add chicken.

Dumplings:
3 cups flour
1-1/2 teaspoons salt
1/4 teaspoon pepper
5 tablespoons shortening
2 eggs, well beaten
3/4 to 1 cup milk

1. To make dumplings, mix flour, salt and pepper. Cut in shortening. Add eggs and milk.
2. Working with half the dough at a time, place on well floured board. Knead in flour until dough is of a non-sticky consistency.
3. Roll to 1/4 inch thickness and cut in 1 to 2-inch squares or cut with a heart shaped cookie cutter.
4. Drop into boiling broth and simmer 15 to 20 minutes or until tender.

Makes 8 servings.

gepa's vegetable soup

When I was a little girl, my dad would make this soup for us.
He didn't use a recipe and never wrote it down for me. What I
remember clearly is that he would begin with the ground beef
and end with the cabbage—all the in-between vegetables would
vary according to what was available or "on hand". It's a fast
soup to make. You'll be amazed at how easy it is to put together
such a delicious "good for you" meal with such ease — and still
have time to mix up a batch of cornbread to go with it!

1 pound lean ground beef
1 medium onion, chopped
4 to 6 cloves garlic
4 carrots, sliced
6 ribs celery, sliced
1 medium sweet potato, chopped
1 can tomatoes, chopped
1 medium cabbage, chopped
1 to 2 cups potatoes, cubed
12 cups beef broth
2 bay leaves
Salt and black pepper, freshly ground, to taste

❶ Saute meat, onion, garlic until browned.
❷ Add celery and carrots and saute for 5 minutes. Add remaining
   ingredients and cook for 1 hour. Taste for salt and pepper.

Makes 24 cups.

creamy corn and green chili soup

My goal here was to make a creamy soup — not too complex — with just a hint of light and mild flavors to enhance the good taste of corn. Even with the addition of the green chilies, this soup is very light and mild tasting. Pay close attention to the garnish ideas — they are all good possibilities for embellishing!

1 medium onion, chopped
2 tablespoons butter
2 cloves garlic, sliced
4 cups frozen corn (or fresh corn removed from cob)
2-1/2 cups milk
2 teaspoons salt
1/2 cup cilantro leaves
1 cup canned green chilies
1 tablespoon sugar

❶ In medium saucepan, cook onion, butter and garlic until onions are tender.
❷ Add corn, milk and salt. Bring to a boil, then reduce heat and cover. Cook gently for 15 minutes.
❸ Add cilantro, green chilies and sugar. Cook for 2 to 3 minutes. Remove from heat and puree. Reheat and serve.

Makes 6 cups.

NOTE:

PURPLE CHIVE BLOSSOMS

WOULD BE PRETTY

ON TOP — OR CRIMSON

PINEAPPLE SAGE

BLOSSOMS.

chive blossom

GARNISH:

GRATED COTIJA CHEESE,

TORTILLA NOODLES (THIS

SECTION) OR PEPITAS

(SEE APPETIZERS)

jalapeño sweet potato soup

This is another variation of our popular Jalapeño Potato Soup from **The Peach Tree Tea Room Cookbook,** this time with sweet potatoes. It's already a new favorite whenever we serve it in our Tea Room.

3 slices bacon, finely chopped
I medium onion, chopped
2 tablespoons butter
3 cloves garlic, sliced
4 pounds sweet potatoes, peeled and cubed
8 cups chicken broth
I/4 cup pickled jalapeños, coarsely chopped
2 tablespoons jalapeño juice
I teaspoon comino
I/4 teaspoon baking soda
I/2 cup cilantro leaves
I-I/2 cups milk
I teaspoon salt
I teaspoon black pepper, freshly ground

❶ In large stock pot, saute bacon and onion in butter until just tender. Add garlic and cook about 2 more minutes.

❷ Add sweet potatoes, chicken broth, pickled jalapeños, jalapeño juice and comino. Cover and cook until potatoes are tender, about 20 to 30 minutes.

❸ When done, add soda, cilantro and milk. Coarsely mash potatoes with a potato masher.

❹ Stir well and taste for salt and pepper. Simmer for 15 minutes, stirring frequently.

Makes I4 cups.

GARNISH:

SOUR CREAM AND 3 OR 4 FRESH JALAPEÑOS, CUT IN THIN LENGTHWISE STRIPS - PEPITAS (SEE APPETIZER) ARE GOOD, TOO!

Late August

A great new potato soup for us – really a variation of the ever popular Jalapeño Potato Soup in our first cookbook. Canned green chiles work really well for this recipe, but if you roast your own fresh chiles you will be rewarded with wonderfully intense flavors.

We have cherished memories of our trips to Colorado and New Mexico in late August. It's my favorite time to go so we can cool off from the long hot Texas summer! On the way home, what is really fun for me is to stop and buy fresh roasted chiles from the vendors with their open air roasters. Nothing can compare with the flavor — and the fragrance that fills the fresh mountain air. It's part of my effort to experience the moment for as long as I can!!

roasted green chile and potato soup

4 cloves fresh garlic, sliced
1 medium onion, chopped
1/4 pound bacon, sliced
2-1/2 pounds red potatoes, 1 inch cubes (about 5 medium sized potatoes)
6 cups chicken broth
1 teaspoon comino
2 cups green chiles, roasted and peeled
1 pinch baking soda to prevent curdling
1 cup evaporated milk
Salt and pepper, freshly ground, to taste

❶ In a large stock pot, saute garlic, onion, and bacon until onions are just tender.

❷ Add potatoes, chicken broth, and comino. Cover and cook until potatoes are tender, about 20 to 30 minutes.

❸ When done, add green chiles, soda and evaporated milk. Coarsely mash potatoes with a potato masher.

❹ Stir well and taste for salt and pepper. Simmer for 15 minutes, stirring frequently. Garnish with a dollop of sour cream and finely chopped green onions, or grated Cotija cheese and chopped Pepitas (see Appetizers).

Serves 8 to 10

NOTE:

THIS CAN BE ADJUSTED -

IF YOU HAPPEN TO GET

A BATCH OF VERY HOT

PEPPERS - USE LESS!

GARNISH:

SOUR CREAM AND

CHOPPED GREEN

ONIONS.

butternut squash, chicken and wild rice

This soup is lovely to look at and just as good to eat! The recipe is perfect just as it is written and would also be good using sweet potatoes or fresh pumpkin in place of the butternut squash. It has gotten raves in our Tea Room.

1 4-ounce package pure wild rice
4 ribs celery, sliced
1 large onion, chopped
2 tablespoons olive oil
10 medium garlic cloves, minced
1-1/2 tablespoons comino
1-1/2 tablespoons oregano
1 tablespoon black pepper, freshly ground
2 quarts homemade or canned chicken broth
1 medium butternut squash (about 1-1/2 to 2 pounds), peeled and cubed
2 cups red potatoes, cubed
3 cups cooked chicken, chopped
Salt to taste

1. Cook rice according to package directions.
2. Saute celery and onion in olive oil until transparent.
3. Add garlic, comino, oregano and black pepper. Stirring until fragrant.
4. Add chicken broth and bring to a boil.
5. Add butternut squash and potatoes. Cook until squash and potatoes are tender but firm, add chicken and rice and taste for seasonings. Add salt if necessary.

Makes 12 to 14 cups.

Beautiful Soup!

pinto bean soup

Our fresh Tea Room Pico de Gallo is the inspiration for this popular soup — so much flavor and it's fat free!

4 cups pinto beans
1/2 cup cilantro, chopped
2 tablespoons jalapeños
1 cup carrots, sliced
1 cup onions, chopped
1 tablespoon garlic, chopped
1 tablespoon comino
12 cups chicken broth
1 teaspoon salt

❶ Combine all ingredients in a large stock pot. Cover and cook 3 to 4 hours on low heat until beans are very soft. (This also can be done the way we do it in the Tea Room. Use a large crockpot and cook all night on a low heat setting.)

❷ When beans are done, puree in food processor. (Be very careful here, as hot liquid will expand).

❸ Place beans back in pot and thin to desired consistency with extra chicken broth. Taste for salt. Reheat and serve with a big spoonful of Tea Room Pico de Gallo (see Breakfast) and a sprinkle of grated Cotija cheese.

Serves 12 to 16.

pueblo pork stew

The colors, tastes and textures of the pretty garnish are a very
important part of this delicious soup — rather like a little salad on
top of the hearty chile flavored broth. You could serve garnishes in
individual bowls and let your guests choose one or all!

4 garlic cloves, divided use
6 cups water
2 cups chicken broth
2 pounds country-style pork ribs
1/2 teaspoon dried oregano leaves
1 ounce dried New Mexico red chiles (about 3 chiles)
3/4 cup boiling-hot water
1/4 large white onion, cut in chunks
1 30-ounce can white hominy
2 teaspoons salt

1. Slice 2 cloves garlic. In an 8-quart heavy kettle, boil water and
   broth with sliced garlic and pork. Skim surface and add oregano.
   Gently simmer pork uncovered, until tender, about 1-1/2 hours.
2. While cooking pork, soak chiles in boiling hot water for
   30 minutes. Turn them occasionally.
3. Remove stems and seeds from chiles. Puree chiles, onion with
   soaking liquid, reserved garlic and salt - until smooth.
4. Remove pork to cutting board. Reserve liquid and add enough
   water to make 8 cups. Shred pork.
5. Drain and rinse hominy. Return pork to broth mixture. Add
   chile sauce and hominy. Simmer for 30 minutes, and add more
   salt if needed.

Makes 12 cups.

GARNISH:

THINLY SHREDDED

GREEN CABBAGE,

TORTILLA NOODLES

(SEE THIS SECTION),

LIME WEDGES, DICED

RADISHES, CHOPPED

ONION, AVOCADO.

sweet potato corn chowder

3 slices bacon, coarsely chopped
I cup onion, coarsely chopped
I cup red pepper, coarsely chopped
I cup leek, coarsely chopped
I teaspoon fresh thyme or I/2 teaspoon dried thyme leaves
I teaspoon fresh marjoram, chopped, or I/2 teaspoon dried
marjoram leaves
I/2 teaspoon salt
I/2 teaspoon black pepper, freshly ground
2 medium-size sweet potatoes, (I pound), peeled, I/2 inch
chunks
I cup fresh or frozen corn
6 cups chicken broth
3 cups water, divided use
2 teaspoons cornstarch
I/2 cup half and half or milk
2 cups cooked chicken, cut in chunks

❶ In stock pot, saute bacon over medium heat until crisp and
browned. Remove bacon and set aside.
❷ Add onion, red pepper, leek, thyme, marjoram, salt and pepper
to bacon drippings. Saute for 10 minutes, stirring occasionally.
❸ Add sweet potatoes, corn, chicken broth and 2-1/2 cups water to
mixture in stock pot. Cook until sweet potatoes are tender - 15
to 20 minutes. Mix cornstarch and I/2 cup water and stir into
soup. Heat to boiling, stirring constantly and cook until
thickened.
❹ Reduce heat to low, stir in half and half or milk, bacon and
cooked chicken.

Makes 10 cups.

salads

my favorite ingredients

KOSHER SALT OR COARSE SEA SALT: I love using Kosher Salt, and it's the only kind of salt I buy. - It has a cleaner taste, not as dense as the table salt that we are all accustomed to using. The little crystals also give a pretty sparkling appearance. The flavor of Kosher Salt is more intense so when measuring it you can always start with less than is required in a recipe - more can be added if you like.

You are the salt of the earth   Matt. 5:13

GARLIC: I make a point to have at least 6 pods of fresh garlic on my kitchen counter at all times! I can't imagine life without garlic. Now when I cook I hardly ever mince garlic. I love the taste and I'm glad for the good report that garlic has received for its health benefits! And, I slice it so I can enjoy seeing it. Garlic is one of my favorite ingredients and I especially like the way the little slices look in a dish. Also, by slicing rather than mincing, there is less moisture released and it is less likely to burn when a recipe requires sauteing.

I have great compassion for the Israelites when I read how they tired of the Manna that God provided for them on their journey to the promised land and they wanted to go back to the leeks and garlic in Eygpt — remember?

So I feel very blessed to be able to use garlic as much as my heart desires. If you own my first book - **The Peach Tree Tea Room Cookbook**, you will note that most recipes call for 1 clove of garlic — and the recipes in this book begin with 2 to 3 cloves. Be BOLD and Enjoy!!

BALSAMIC VINEGAR: I first became aware of balsamic vinegar when a long time friend served it over fresh strawberries. If you've never tried strawberries this way you're in for a special taste treat.

Simply sprinkle the berries with a little (1 to 2 teaspoons) bit of vinegar, then sugar, if desired. Wait for about a half hour — stir and serve! Balsamic vinegar accentuates the flavor. The result is such that the berries taste even more like strawberries!

Since that first encounter I have grown to depend on balsamic vinegar as one of my favorites for my salads. I love the flavor blend of fresh greens, tossed with apples or pears, pecans, blue cheese and balsamic vinegar.

I use it also to finish off my roasted vegetables. It really doesn't take much — just a sprinkle to enhance and complement the good vegetable flavors.

COLD PRESSED SALAD OILS: I go to the health food store to shop for my salad dressing oils. They are cold pressed which means that the ingredients are not processed with heat to extract the oil, but rather are simply pressed.

These oils give a fresh clean taste to my salads, and I'm secure in knowing that many of the nutrients have not been destroyed.

For everyday salads, I especially like canola, safflower or sunflower oil. Walnut, pumpkin seed and sesame can be interesting ones to try, too.

fruit salad dressings

Here are three very simple dressings that I like to use on fruit. The flavors are gentle and are just enough to enhance the flavor of good fresh fruit. There are no set amounts of ingredients — just have fun and create!

YOGURT & HONEY
Blend honey into nonfat yogurt just a little at a time until you get the taste you like. Good on fruit with toasted pecans sprinkled on top.

YOGURT, ORANGE JUICE & CHOPPED MINT LEAVES
Blend orange juice and mint leaves into yogurt just a little at a time until you get the taste you like.

HONEY & LIME
Drizzle honey over fruit then squeeze fresh lime juice — the flavors are a delicious complement to one another.

SOUR CREAM & BROWN SUGAR
Place a dollop of sour cream over fresh fruit and sprinkle with brown sugar or maple sugar. Try this on watermelon. You will be surprised at how good it is!

lemon maple vinaigrette

Especially good over a salad of romaine lettuce, cucumbers, sliced red peppers and fresh grated Parmesan. I make this dressing often at home for Hector and me — he says it's his favorite!

2 cloves garlic
1 teaspoon Kosher salt
Juice of 1 lemon
2 tablespoons maple syrup
Black pepper, freshly ground
4 tablespoons Canola oil

❶ Place garlic cloves and Kosher salt in wooden salad bowl and mash with a wooden spoon until it forms a paste.
❷ Add lemon juice, maple syrup, pepper and oil, and stir to mix well.

Makes 1/3 cup — enough for 4 dinner-size salads.

NOTE:

KOSHER SALT IS COARSER

AND LIGHTER THAN

REGULAR TABLE SALT.

I PREFER USING IT FOR

ALL OF MY COOKING, BUT

IF YOU DON'T HAVE IT

JUST USE HALF AS MUCH

OF THE REGULAR KIND,

WHICH IS MUCH DENSER.

TRY THIS DRESSING

POURED OVER

STEAMED CABBAGE —

IT'S REALLY GOOD

SERVED WITH PORK.

lemon salad dressing

Made with low fat yogurt this is a light dressing for fruit — Green apples, grapes and slices of poached chicken and toasted almonds on salad greens would be a nice summer lunch!

1/2 cup sour cream or yogurt
2 tablespoons lemon juice
1 teaspoon sugar
1/2 teaspoon salt
1/2 teaspoon black pepper, freshly ground
2 teaspoons fresh lemon balm, chopped
2 teaspoons fresh lemon verbena, chopped
1 tablespoon walnuts, chopped

Place in small bowl and mix well until smooth.

Makes 1/2 cup.

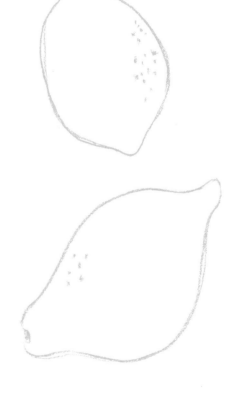

lemon

blue cheese lite

Delicious light nonfat salad dressing — over baked potatoes, and a terrific dip for fresh veggies!

1 cup low fat cottage cheese
1/3 cup buttermilk
1/4 cup blue cheese
1 teaspoon dill or parsley, chopped
1 teaspoon black pepper, freshly ground

Blend cheeses and buttermilk till smooth. Add dill and pepper. Serve.

Makes 1-1/2 cups.

NOTE:

PARSLEY, GARLIC CHIVES

OR DILL ARE GOOD

CHOICES FOR THIS OIL.

herb oil

I love to put this in a nice bottle in my fridge — it's a very pretty way to dress up summer salad plates — just drizzle a few drops on the outer rim of the plate — it's tasty too!

2 cups fresh herb leaves
1-1/2 cups grape seed oil
1/2 cup olive oil

❶ Blanch herbs in boiling salted water. Shock in ice water. Drain.
❷ Place in blender with oils - puree until dark green. About 3 minutes.
❸ Refrigerate for 1 day - Strain.
❹ Chill.

Makes 2 cups.

french lentil salad

I love the flavor and texture of French lentils. They are dark green and very tiny, so different from the brown lentils I have used for soup. This is a nice salad to have in the fridge for the hot summer months - good to serve on a pretty lettuce leaf with grilled meats - and nutritious on its own to be the main event for a light lunch. The chopped red onions and peppers and parsley give the salad a colorful confetti look and a tasty crunchy texture.

NOTE:

CRUMBLED FETA CHEESE
SPRINKLED OVER THE
SALAD IS PRETTY AND A
VERY TASTY ADDITION —
FRESHLY GRATED
PARMESAN OR ASIAGO
CHEESE IS ALSO A GREAT
GARNISH!

6 cups water
2 teaspoons salt
2 cups green lentils, pick through and rinse
1 or 1-1/2 medium red onions, finely diced (1-1/2 to 2 cups)
1 medium red or yellow pepper, finely diced (1-1/2 to 2 cups) or cut into tiny slivers for a different eye appeal - if the mood strikes you
4 teaspoons balsamic vinegar
1/4 cup olive oil
1/4 cup canola oil
4 cloves garlic, finely minced
6 tablespoons lemon juice
1/2 cup Italian parsley, finely chopped
1 teaspoon black pepper, freshly ground
1 tablespoon salt

❶ Bring water to boil with 2 teaspoons salt, add lentils.
❷ Cook for 20 to 25 minutes until lentils are soft. Be careful not to overcook, as they will become mushy. Pour lentils into colander. Rinse quickly with cold water to prevent more cooking.
❸ Toss with remaining ingredients and chill for several hours or overnight.

Makes 8 cups.

everyday at home
salad dressing

This is another of the dressings I often make at home. I like the sweet flavor of the Balsamic vinegar — especially when I add apples or oranges to the greens. It's also nice with toasted nuts sprinkled on top!

2 cloves garlic
2 teaspoons sugar
2 or 3 tablespoons balsamic vinegar
1/2 teaspoon black pepper, freshly ground
4 tablespoons canola oil
1/2 teaspoons Kosher salt, or to taste

❶ Place garlic cloves and sugar in wooden salad bowl and mash with a wooden spoon until it forms a paste

❷ Add balsamic vinegar, pepper and oil, and stir to mix well. Taste and add salt, if desired.

Makes 1/3 cup.

4 STEPS TO SALAD MAKING.

Several years ago I was invited to become a member of Les Dames de Escoffier in San Antonio. It is an international organization of women who have centered their careers around food, and the purpose is to seek ways to encourage other women who desire to pursue a food related career. We're a small chapter and I love our get togethers. Business meetings are always followed by something good to eat. One of the most memorable to me was this delightful salad served by Cynthia Guido, who is very talented and creative. I am grateful to her for her generous sharing of this very special recipe. She serves these chiles stuffed with guacamole salad. You will LOVE them!!

chile anchos en escabeche

6 ancho chiles, dried, cleaned and seeded
I/2 cup canola oil
I medium white onion, sliced
I/2 cup orange juice
I cup apple cider vinegar
I pound piloncillo or dark brown sugar
Salt and pepper to taste

❶ Slit open the chiles lengthwise with kitchen shears, remove seeds (leave stem intact), remove veins. Rinse and let dry.

❷ Fry chiles very briefly in hot oil. Drain, reserving oil to use to fry onions until tender.

❸ In sauce pan, bring to boil — orange juice, vinegar, sugar, salt and pepper. Cook briefly at lower temperature. Remove from heat.

❹ Add chiles and onion to this sweet-sour marinade, and let the chiles macerate until they are soft — preferable overnight.

❺ Stuff chiles as desired.

Makes 6 servings.

♡ NOTE:

WE DEVELOPED THIS

RECIPE TO SERVE IN

OUR TEA ROOM. THE

ADDITION OF LIME

JUICE AND CILANTRO

ENHANCES THE FLAVOR.

IT BECOMES A GREAT

TOPPING FOR CHALUPAS

OR TACOS OR FILLING FOR

THE CHILE ANCHOS EN

ESCABECHE (SEE THIS

SECTION).

guacamole

6 to 8 avocados, peeled and seeded
1 tablespoon lemon or lime juice
2 to 4 tablespoons jalapeños, coarsely chopped
1/4 cup picante salsa
1/2 cup cilantro, chopped
1 tablespoon garlic, finely minced
4 tablespoons onion, finely chopped
1/2 teaspoon salt
1/2 teaspoon black pepper, freshly ground

❶ Mash avocado with potato masher to desired consistency.
   (I like mine chunky, not too smooth)
❷ Stir in remaining ingredients and mix throughly.
   Taste for salt and add more if desired

4 to 6 servings

tortilla noodles

We have been making these tortilla "noodles" for years to complement our Tortilla Soup which is served every week in the Tea Room. The noodles are so good we use them to accent other dishes as well. Make as many as you like!

Corn tortillas
Canola oil, 1/4 inch in pan

Slice tortillas into thin strips and fry in hot canola oil until crisp and golden. Drain on paper towels.

MAKING SALAD LESSON!

arugula chicken salad with lemon maple vinaigrette

Maple is becoming a very important ingredient for me — I love its subtle flavor. This salad has an interesting mix of flavors and texture. When I was a young girl, learning to make salads with my mother, I was told never to cut lettuce, but to tear the leaves. My mother also taught me that in art and design you must study to know the rules before you can break them — I break the "lettuce rule" here and the outcome is fresh tasting and most delicious!

2 chicken breasts, pounded thin and sauteed in olive oil, sliced into thin strips
3 cups arugula, sliced
3 cups romaine, sliced
I cup corn Tortilla Noodles (see this section)
I/2 small green apple, unpeeled & chopped
I ear corn, kernels, removed, uncooked
2 ribs celery, sliced on diagonal
2 recipes Lemon Maple Vinaigrette (see this section)

Combine salad ingredients and toss well with Lemon Maple Vinaigrette. Serve.

Makes 6 to 8 servings.

holiday chicken salad

I make Cranberry Salsa to sell in the Tea Room all during the holidays from Thanksgiving until Christmas and New Years. It's the salsa that led me to create this very pretty and festive salad. We place a scoop on salad greens and sprinkle toasted walnuts on top and around the plate.

6 cups cooked chicken breast, cut into 1-inch cubes
1 cup Orange Roasted Garlic Mayo (see this section)
1-1/2 cups celery, cut into thin diagonal slices
1-1/2 cups Granny Smith apples, diced
1 cup green onions, 2 inch slices
1 cup Cranberry Salsa (see Appetizers)

In large mixing bowl combine all ingredients and toss well. Serve chilled.

Makes 10 to 12 servings.

VARIATION:

THIS IS A DELICIOUS SALAD TO MAKE AT OTHER TIMES OF THE YEAR WHEN CRANBERRIES ARE NOT IN SEASON - SIMPLY OMIT THE CRANBERRY SALSA — IF DESIRED, YOU CAN ADD 2 TABLESPOONS CHOPPED CILANTRO, 1-1/2 CUPS DRIED CRANBERRIES AND 1 TABLESPOON CURRY POWDER.

almond chicken salad

This is a very tasty salad - good on a bed of greens or as a sandwich on a crusty croissant. I've also served it stuffed into a roasted chile poblano pepper.

6 cups cooked chicken breast, cut into 1/2 inch cubes
2 cups celery, thinly sliced, about 1/4 inch
1 cup red onions, finely chopped
3 green onions, finely chopped
4 garlic cloves, minced
1 cup mayonnaise (good quality prepared) or Peach Tree Herb Mayonnaise (see Sandwiches)
3/4 cup sour cream
1 tablespoon fresh Mexican Marigold Mint, finely chopped
2 teaspoons salt
1 teaspoon pepper, freshly ground
3/4 cup golden raisins
1-1/2 cups sliced almonds, toasted

Place all ingredients in mixing bowl. Toss lightly until combined. Refrigerate until ready to serve.

Makes 12 cups.

chicken and wild rice salad

What a delightful way to enjoy your complex carbohydrates. I like
to serve this salad in a crisp green bibb lettuce leaf garnished with
orange slices and a sprinkle of toasted walnuts.

2 cups cooked chicken, thinly sliced
2-4 ounce packages wild rice, cooked according to directions
(5 cups cooked)
1 cup celery, thinly sliced on diagonal
1 cup red or green grapes, sliced in half
1 cup Granny Smith apples, very thinly sliced, unpeeled
1 cup walnuts, toasted, chopped coarsely
1/4 cup green onion, finely sliced
1/2 teaspoon salt
2 teaspoons sugar
2 cloves garlic, minced
Juice and zest of one orange
1/2 cup canola oil
1 teaspoon soy sauce

Combine all ingredients. Serve immediately on fresh salad greens
or serve chilled.

Makes 10 cups.

insalata pilaf

It would be difficult to top this salad for its delicious mix of flavors and nutritional value. It is rich in vitamins and complex carbohydrates. Serve over a bed of tasty salad greens, or use it to fill either fresh summer home grown tomatoes or peppers. Just mix and enjoy!

1 cup cooked wild rice
1 cup cooked brown rice
1/3 cup cooked barley
1/2 cup soaked bulgur (cracked wheat)
2 cups toasted pecan halves
1-1/2 cups fresh corn kernels, uncooked
1 large tomato, peeled, seeded and chopped
1 bunch green onions, chopped (including green tops)
1/2 bunch fresh parsley

Dressing:
1 cup rice vinegar
1/2 cup peanut oil
Salt to taste

❶ In a large bowl place all salad ingredients.
❷ To prepare dressing combine all ingredients and whisk until mixed.
❸ Pour dressing over salad mixture and toss to combine well. Serve on a bed of mixed salad greens.

Makes 8 to 10 servings.

maple marinated shrimp salad with watercress

This is a wonderful and refreshing salad to serve for a light lunch. A delicious "add to" would be a cup of soup and corn muffins. It sells out very fast when we feature it as a Tea Room special.

1 pound shrimp, boiled, shelled and chilled
1 red pepper, sliced thinly
1 cup fresh corn kernels
2 recipes Lemon Maple Vinaigrette (see this section)
2 cups romaine lettuce, chopped coarsely
2 cups watercress, chopped coarsely
1 cup Tortilla Noodles (see this section)
1 cup black beans, cooked and rinsed

❶ Place shrimp, red peppers and corn in a bowl with half the Lemon Maple Vinaigrette, let marinate for about 10 minutes.
❷ Toss together the lettuce, watercress, remaining dressing, and Tortilla Noodles.
❸ Place on four individual plates - top each with shrimp mixture - sprinkle border of plate with black beans and garnish with sliced avocado.

Makes 4 servings.

wilted spinach & bacon salad

I learned how to make this salad from watching my mother when I was little. It's so simple and good. Every time I make it I wonder why I don't do it more often!

4 ounces lean bacon, cut into 1" strips (4 strips)
2 to 4 cloves garlic, sliced lengthwise
1 teaspoon sugar
1/2 teaspoon black pepper, freshly ground
2 to 3 tablespoons olive oil
1 tablespoon balsamic vinegar
1/2 pound fresh spinach

❶ Saute bacon in small skillet. Pour off grease.
❷ Add garlic - saute until light brown. Add sugar, pepper and stir until sugar dissolves. Add olive oil and vinegar.
❸ Add spinach - stir until just wilted.
❹ Serve immediately.

Makes 2 servings.

Eat your spinach!

hot potato salad

NOTE:

IF USING LARGER

POTATOES, CUT IN

QUARTERS OR BITE

SIZE PIECES.

This is another salad I remember watching my mother make when I was a little girl. I always liked to sneak bites of the bacon before supper was served and eat it first — I still do! Some habits are hard to break.

1-1/2 pounds small whole red potatoes
1 tablespoon salt
4 ounces (4 strips) lean bacon, cut into 1/2" strips
3 cloves garlic, sliced
1 cup green onions, in 1" slices
1 cup celery, cut diagonally into 1/4" slices
3 tablespoons olive oil
1 tablespoon red wine vinegar or apple cider vinegar
Salt and black pepper, freshly ground, to taste

❶ In a large saucepan, cover the potatoes with cold water, add salt and bring to a boil over high heat. Reduce the heat and simmer until tender, about 20 minutes.

❷ While potatoes are cooking, saute bacon, pour off excess grease. Add garlic and saute until browned.

❸ In salad bowl, mix green onion, celery, olive oil, vinegar and salt and pepper. Mix all with hot potatoes and bacon. Keep at room temperature for about 30 minutes stirring a few times before serving.

Makes 4 to 6 servings.

NOTE:

THIS DRESSING IS

EXCELLENT ON SALADS

AND CAN BE STORED IN

THE REFRIGERATOR IN AN

AIR TIGHT CONTAINER

tarragon sherry asparagus marinade

This delicious dish appeared on my kitchen counter one evening when the Schmidts came over to taste the bounty of a day of recipe testing. It's too good not to share! A lovely meal would be this asparagus served with the Chicken Milanesa - and for dessert, Lemon Lush Pie!

2 pounds fresh asparagus, blanched

Dressing:
1 to 2 teaspoons dried tarragon, or 1 to 2 tablespoons fresh, minced tarragon
6 cornichons, finely minced
2 cups extra virgin olive oil
1/3 cup fresh lemon juice
1/3 cup sherry wine vinegar (don't substitute)
1 tablespoon Dijon mustard
Salt and black pepper, freshly ground, to taste

❶ Blanch asparagus by placing in boiling water for 30 seconds or so. Then immerse in ice water and drain.
❷ Combine all dressing ingredients in food processor and process until well combined.
❸ Pour over asparagus right before serving (asparagus turns dark if you apply it in advance.)

Makes 6 to 8 servings.

breads

Communion

I HAD AN INSIGHT AT CHURCH EARLIER THIS YEAR

when I was taking communion at the altar rail. I was the last one on the row

to receive and as the priest drew nearer I heard him repeating over and over

as he placed the wafer into the open palms:

> *"The body of Christ – the feast of heaven. The body of Christ –*
> *the feast of heaven. The body of Christ – the feast of heaven.*

My attention was engaged as never before — maybe, because until recently
I've not given such thought to heaven — and what it must be like for those
who reside there.

For several hours I reflected.

I then realized with intense clarity, that it is we who believe who are the
Body of Christ. When we arrive there to join the Eternal Feast there will be
a reunion with those we love and miss. We, in Christ, will feast... laughing
and rejoicing as never before. I now believe that when my relationships are
pleasing to God — it is just like a huge appetizer to the feasting to come!

LOVE IS THE CONTINUAL FEAST.

NOTE:

THIS RECIPE WILL BE

USED AS A REFERENCE

FOR THE JALAPEÑO

CHEESE BREAD, SUN

DRIED TOMATO PESTO

BREAD AND THE ROASTED

RED PEPPER AND

GARLIC BREAD.

peach tree country french bread

Every morning in our Tea Room kitchen we begin with the mixing of this wonderful basic yeast dough. Since opening our Tea Room doors 14 years ago, this bread has been at the heart of our menu selections. I'm not sure when it happened, but over the years since the first Tea Room cookbook, rolled oats were added to our recipe which gives our loaves a lighter texture. From this recipe come the popular and beautiful breads which we serve and sell in our deli-bakery. The recipes that follow give you the ingredients and the techniques so that you too can make the savory filled breads in your home.

This basic French dough also makes a delicious loaf just as it is. It is the bread that we marinate for our Peachy French Toast (see Breakfast). And for tea sandwiches we bake the bread in our heart shaped pans and slice it thin. For our delicious Crostini we make long skinny loaves, slice thinly, and toast the small slices to hold savory toppings listed in the Appetizer section.

Have fun with this recipe - it's my hope that mastering it, will lead you into some exciting creative adventures of your own.

1 tablespoon active dry yeast
1-1/2 teaspoons sugar
1-1/2 cups lukewarm water
3 cups unbleached flour
1/2 cup whole wheat flour
1/2 cup rolled oats
1-1/2 teaspoons salt
Oil, enough to brush on dough
Egg wash: 1 egg beaten with 1 tablespoon water

1. Dissolve yeast and sugar in lukewarm water.
2. Combine 2 cups unbleached flour, whole wheat flour, oats and salt. Add to the yeast mixture, stirring well with wooden spoon. (This step can also be done in a food processor using a dough blade.)
3. Knead the dough on a lightly floured board gradually adding last cup of unbleached flour until it is no longer sticky. Place dough in oiled bowl; brush top with oil. Cover with plastic wrap or a clean kitchen towel and let rise until doubled, about one hour.
4. After dough has doubled in size, punch down and turn out onto floured board. Divide into 2 parts. (See our Forming the Loaf section.)
5. Place loaves seam side down on greased cookie sheet that has been sprinkled with cornmeal. Cover and let rise about 30 minutes. Using serrated knife, make shallow diagonal slices on top of each loaf. Brush Egg wash on each loaf.
6. Bake in preheated oven at 400 degrees for 20 to 25 minutes or until golden.

Makes 2 large loaves.

RISING BREAD DOUGH

The Tea Room's filled breads

jalapeño cheese bread

NOTE:

THIS IS JUST ONE OF THE

VARIATIONS YOU CAN

MAKE WITH THE PEACH

TREE COUNTRY FRENCH

BREAD RECIPE.

This is one of the first filled breads we created in the Tea Room, and for many of our customers it's still a favorite — Monterey Jack cheese, pickled jalapeños and a little comino - delicioso!!

I recipe Peach Tree Country French Bread

Filling:
3 teaspoons ground comino
4 tablespoons Monterey Jack cheese, grated
4 tablespoons jalapeños, sliced

Egg wash: I egg beaten with I tablespoon water

Topping:
2 tablespoons comino
8 tablespoons Monterey Jack cheese, grated

Refer to Peach Tree Country French Bread recipe for steps 1,2, and 3 and then proceed as follows:

❹ After dough has doubled in size, punch down and turn out onto floured board. Divide into 2 parts. Pat each portion into a rectangular shape about 3/4 inch thick. Sprinkle comino over dough, then cheese and jalapeños. Roll into loaf shape, sealing in the filling (See our Forming the Loaf section).

❺ Place loaves seam side down on greased cookie sheet that has been sprinkled with cornmeal. Cover and let rise about 30 minutes. Using serrated knife, make shallow diagonal slices on top of each loaf. Brush Egg wash on each loaf.

❻ Topping: Sprinkle comino, then cheese over each loaf.

❼ Bake in a preheated 400 degrees in oven, 20 to 25 minutes.

Makes 2 large loaves.

NOTE:

WE USE SUN DRIED

TOMATO PESTO (SEE

APPETIZERS) FOR THIS

BREAD EACH DAY IN

THE TEA ROOM — TRY

OTHER PESTOS AS WELL

AND CREATE YOUR

OWN VERSION!

sun dried tomato pesto bread

1 recipe Peach Tree Country French Bread

Filling:
6 tablespoons Sun Dried Tomato Pesto (see Appetizers)
6 tablespoons Parmesan cheese, freshly grated
4 tablespoons walnuts, coarsely chopped
Oil, enough to brush on dough

Egg wash: 1 egg beaten with 1 tablespoon water

Topping:
6 tablespoons Parmesan cheese, freshly grated

Refer to Peach Tree Country French Bread recipe for steps 1, 2, and 3 and then proceed as follows:

4 After dough has doubled in size, punch down and turn out onto floured board. Divide into 2 parts. Pat each portion into a rectangular shape about 3/4 inch thick. Spread pesto, then sprinkle with cheese and walnuts. Roll into loaf shape, sealing in the filling. (see our Forming the Loaf section.)

5 Place loaves seam side down on greased cookie sheet that has been sprinkled with cornmeal. Cover and let rise about 30 minutes. Using serrated knife, make shallow diagonal slices on top of each loaf. Brush Egg wash on each loaf.

6 Topping: Sprinkle Parmesan on each loaf.

7 Bake in preheated oven at 400 degrees for 20 to 25 minutes or until golden.

Makes 2 large loaves.

forming the loaf series

I LOVE THE FACT THAT A LOAF OF BREAD BEGINS WITH THE MOST BASIC INGREDIENTS—FLOUR, WATER, YEAST, SUGAR AND SALT. WHAT TAKES PLACE IN THE PROCESS OF BECOMING A LOAF IS AWESOME TO BEHOLD.

NOTE:

WE USE LOTS OF ASIAGO

CHEESE IN OUR TEA

ROOM RECIPES — IT'S

THE CHEESE THAT WE USE

ON OUR CAESAR SALAD.

IT'S ALSO GOOD ON

PASTAS AND IN OUR

BREADS AND IS SOME-

WHAT LIKE A SOFT

VERSION OF PARMESAN

IN FLAVOR.

roasted red pepper and garlic bread

Roasted red peppers, roasted garlic and Asiago cheese folded into our Peach Tree Country French bread — it's good with everything!

I recipe Peach Tree Country French Bread

Filling:
4 tablespoons Roasted Garlic cloves (see Side Dishes)
4 tablespoons Asiago cheese, grated
2/3 cup Roasted Red Peppers (see Side Dishes), sliced
Oil - enough to brush on dough

Egg wash: I egg beaten with I tablespoon water

Topping:
8 tablespoons Asiago cheese

Refer to Peach Tree Country French Bread recipe for steps 1,2, and 3 and then proceed as follows:

❹ After dough has doubled in size, punch down and turn out onto floured board. Divide into 2 parts. Pat each portion into a rectangular shape about 3/4 inch thick. Sprinkle with garlic cloves , cheese and roasted peppers. Roll into loaf shape, sealing in the filling. (See our Forming the Loaf section).

❺ Place loaves seam side down on greased cookie sheet that has been sprinkled with cornmeal. Cover and let rise about 30 minutes. Using serrated knife, make shallow diagonal slices on top of each loaf. Brush Egg wash on each loaf.

❻ Topping: Sprinkle cheese on each loaf.

❼ Bake in a preheated 400 degrees in oven, 20 to 25 minutes.

Makes 2 loaves.

's what's on the inside that counts!

We always plan a very special menu to serve for Christmas Nights, a two-night event every December. These are grand evenings. We dress the Tea Room with white tablecloths, roses, candlelight and entertain the guests with carolers from the high school choir.

I created this bread to serve during those special evenings. It's beautiful to look at and oh, so delicious! Just for a change I like to form this dough into round loaves.

apricot pistachio red pepper bread

I tablespoon active dry yeast
I-I/2 teaspoons sugar
I cup lukewarm water
3 cups unbleached flour
I/2 cup whole wheat flour
I/2 cup rolled oats
I-I/2 teaspoons salt
3/4 cup pistachios
3/4 cup Roasted Red Pepper (see Side Dishes), chopped
I cup dried apricots, coarsely chopped
Oil - enough to brush on dough

Egg wash: I egg beaten with I tablespoon water

1. Dissolve yeast and sugar in lukewarm water.

2. Combine 2 cups unbleached flour, whole wheat flour, oats and salt. Mix in pistachios, red peppers and apricots. Add to the yeast mixture, stirring well with wooden spoon. (This can be done in a food processor using a dough blade.) Continue mixing until well blended.

3. Knead the dough on a lightly floured board, gradually adding the last cup of unbleached flour until it is no longer sticky. Place dough in oiled bowl; brush top with oil. Cover with plastic wrap or clean kitchen towel, and let rise until doubled, about one hour.

4. After dough has doubled in size, punch down and turn out onto floured board. Divide into 2 parts. (See our Forming the Loaf section).

5. Place loaves seam side down on greased cookie sheet that has been sprinkled with cornmeal. Cover and let rise about 30 minutes. Using serrated knife, make shallow diagonal slices on top of each loaf. Brush Egg wash on each loaf.

6. Bake in preheated oven at 400 degrees for 20 to 25 minutes or until golden.

Makes 2 large loaves.

texana bread

One of my very favorite breads — this loaf keeps well because of the added olive oil. Note that the ingredients are added into the bread dough during the mixing unlike other filled breads which have the ingredients folded in just before baking. Enjoy!!

1-1/2 cups green onions, sliced
3 tablespoons olive oil
1 tablespoon active dry yeast
1-1/2 teaspoons sugar
1-1/2 cups lukewarm water
3 cups unbleached flour
1/2 cup whole wheat flour
1/2 cup rolled-quick oats
1-1/2 teaspoons salt
1/3 cup Roasted Spiced Pumpkin Seeds (see Appetizers)
1/4 cup Roasted Garlic (see Side Dishes)
1/2 cup Asiago cheese, divided

Egg wash: 1 egg beaten with 1 tablespoon water

Topping:
1/2 cup Asiago cheese
4 tablespoons Roasted Spiced Pumpkin Seeds (see Side Dishes)

without bread, without wine, love is nothing

French Proverb

❶ Saute green onions in olive oil until tender. Let cool.

❷ Dissolve yeast and sugar in lukewarm water.

❸ Combine 2 cups unbleached flour, whole wheat flour, oats and salt. Add to the yeast mixture, stirring well with wooden spoon. (This step can also be done in a food processor using a dough blade.)

❹ Mix onions, Roasted Spiced Pumpkin Seeds and Roasted Garlic in the dough.

❺ Knead the dough on a lightly floured board gradually adding last cup of unbleached flour until it is no longer sticky. Place dough in oiled bowl; brush top with oil. Cover with plastic wrap or a clean kitchen towel and let rise until doubled, about one hour.

❻ After dough has doubled in size, punch down and turn out onto floured board. Divide into 2 parts. Pat each portion into a rectangular shape about 3/4 inch thick. Sprinkle 1/4 cup Asiago cheese on each loaf. Roll into loaf shape, sealing in the cheese. (See our Forming the Loaf section).

❼ Place loaves seam side down on greased cookie sheet that has been sprinkled with cornmeal. Cover and let rise about 30 minutes. Using serrated knife, make shallow diagonal slices on top of each loaf. Brush Egg wash on each loaf.

❽ Topping: Sprinkle remaining 1/2 cup Asiago and pumpkin seeds on top.

❾ Bake in preheated oven at 400 degrees for 20 to 25 minutes or until golden.

Makes 2 loaves.

NOTE:

WHOLE GRAINS TAKE

LONGER TO ABSORB

LIQUID, SO TAKE CARE

TO ADD FLOUR JUST AS

NEEDED. YOU CAN

ALWAYS ADD MORE IF

YOU NEED IT — I FIND

THAT KEEPING A LIGHT

HAND WITH THE FLOUR

IS THE SECRET TO A

LIGHTER AND MORE TEN-

DER LOAF OF BREAD.

super good for you
whole wheat bread

This wonderful bread has become an important part of our Tea Room menu. We serve it toasted for breakfast and at lunchtime with Jalapeño Pimento Cheese and the popular Super Good for You Sandwich (see Sandwiches). It is loaded with ingredients that not only taste good - but also are good for you!

3 cups whole wheat flour, divided
2 tablespoons yeast
1-1/2 cups water
1/2 cup sorghum syrup, molasses or honey
1/2 cup sunflower seeds, coarsely chopped
1/2 cup pumpkin seeds, coarsely chopped
1/4 cup flax seeds
1/2 cup walnuts, coarsely chopped
1/2 cup raisins
1 tablespoon salt
1 cup oats
2 cups milk, scalded and cooled
3 to 4 cups unbleached white flour
Oil - enough to brush on dough
Melted butter - enough to brush on tops

1. In a large bowl, combine 1-1/2 cups whole wheat flour, yeast, water and sorghum syrup, molasses or honey. Mix well and cover with plastic wrap. Let set for at least 2 to 3 hours, or overnight, until a spongy dough forms. Do not refrigerate.
2. Combine seeds, walnuts, raisins, salt, oats and milk. Add to flour-yeast mixture and mix well.
3. Add the unbleached flour and the remaining whole wheat flour. Mix well and turn onto floured board. Knead for 10 minutes until smooth and elastic, adding more flour as needed to prevent sticking.
4. Form dough into large ball. Place dough in oiled bowl and brush the top with oil. Cover with towel and let rise until doubled in size, about 1 hour.
5. Turn onto floured board. Divide dough into 2 parts, form into loaves (see our Forming the Loaf section), and place each in greased bread pan. Let rise again until doubled, about 30 to 45 minutes.
6. Bake in preheated 375 degree oven for 40 to 45 minutes until golden brown. Remove from pans and cool on wire rack. While cooling, brush tops with melted butter.

Makes 2 large loaves.

BREAD IS THE STAFF OF LIFE AND SYMBOL OF NOURISHMENT.

NOTE:

IF YOU HAVE LEFTOVER

ROSEMARY GARLIC

ROASTED POTATOES

(SEE SIDE DISHES) JUST

CHOP COARSELY AND

SUBSTITUTE FOR THE 2

CUPS BOILED POTATOES -

THE ROASTED POTATO

BITS GIVE INTERESTING

TEXTURE TO THE FIN-

ISHED LOAF!

rosemary roasted garlic potato bread

A super delicious bread served in our Tea Room as part of our Fried Green Tomato BLT sandwich (see Sandwiches). It's a beautiful loaf to take on picnics — an abundance of good flavors from summer! Having leftover Rosemary Garlic Roasted Potatoes (see Side Dishes) from the Tea Room resulted in the inspiration for this unusual recipe.

2 tablespoons active dry yeast
2 tablespoons honey
2 cups lukewarm water
2 cups potatoes, boiled and chopped coarsely
1 tablespoon salt
1/4 cup butter
2 tablespoons fresh rosemary leaves
1/2 cup Roasted Garlic (see Side Dishes)
1 cup rye flour
1 cup whole wheat flour
3 cups unbleached flour
1 cup rolled oats
Oil - enough to brush on dough
Melted butter - enough to brush on tops

1. Mix yeast and honey into the lukewarm water. Let it dissolve until bubbly.
2. Combine the potatoes, salt, butter, rosemary, garlic in a large bowl and stir well. Add the yeast mixture and stir well. (This step can also be done in a food processor using a dough blade.)
3. Add flours and oats. Beat well until the dough is smooth. (If you do this in the food processor, the dough will not have to be kneaded by hand.)
4. Knead the dough on a lightly floured board until it is no longer sticky. Place the dough in an oiled bowl; brush top of dough with oil. Cover and let rise until doubled, about 1 to 2 hours depending on how warm your kitchen is.
5. Punch dough down and turn onto floured board. Divide dough into 2 parts, form into loaves, (see our Forming the Loaf section) and place each in greased bread pan. Brush tops with the melted butter. Let rise again until doubled, about 30 to 40 minutes.
6. Bake in preheated 375 degree oven for 40 to 45 minutes until golden brown. Remove from pans and cool on wire rack.

Makes 2 large loaves.

A Tradition

This is a recipe passed down from generation to generation by the German families in the Fredericksburg area. My friend, Loretta, remembers this bread being served at her grandmother's and later at her mother's table. As a child, Loretta remembers it was served with fresh heavy cream and fresh strawberry jam. I think it's a tradition worth preserving — for special occasions, of course!

oma klein's homemade white bread

I package dry yeast
3 tablespoons sugar, divided use
I/2 cup warm water
6 cups flour
2 teaspoons salt
3 tablespoons shortening
I-I/2 cups cold water
Melted butter, enough to brush on finished loaf

1. Dissolve yeast and I tablespoon sugar in warm water. Stir and let sit until foamy.
2. Mix flour, remaining 2 tablespoons sugar, salt and shortening in big bowl until crumbly. Add yeast mixture and cold water. Mix until dough forms together.
3. Turn out on a floured surface and knead until it is smooth and satiny. Place in oiled bowl, cover and let rise in warm place until doubled in bulk.
4. Preheat oven to 350 degrees.
5. Oil 2 medium or I large loaf pan(s). Punch dough down and form into loaf (see our Forming the Loaf section). Put into prepared pan(s), let rise again.
6. Bake 35 to 45 minutes or until brown. Brush with butter and remove from pan.

Makes I to 2 loaves.

NOTE:

THESE ROLLS CAN ALSO

BE FORMED AS CLOVER-

LEAF ROLLS. MAKE THEM

OVERSIZE IN MUFFIN

PANS FOR THAT

INCREDIBLE FARMHOUSE

KITCHEN LOOK!

herbed yeast rolls

Years ago, there was a delightful little restaurant in Fredericksburg. Two of the sweet memories I have of their menu were the home-made ice cream made daily and the delicious herbed yeast rolls. The restaurant has been gone for years and the owners have moved — but the memory of wonderful rolls is mine to keep. In my longing to experience the flavor "one more time", I have developed this variation on the refrigerator yeast rolls that was published in **The Peach Tree Tea Room Cookbook**. It may not be the very same roll but nonetheless they are very good!

2 tablespoons active dry yeast
1/3 cup very warm water
1/2 cup butter
1 cup milk
4-1/4 to 4-3/4 cups unsifted unbleached flour, divided
1/3 cup sugar
2 teaspoons salt
3 large eggs, room temperature
1 package Onion Soup Mix
1/4 cup dried dill weed
Oil - enough to brush dough
Melted butter - enough to brush on rolls

1. Dissolve yeast in warm water. Set aside. In small saucepan over low heat, melt butter in milk.
2. In large bowl, combine 2-3/4 cups flour, sugar, salt, eggs, soup mix, dill weed, dissolved yeast and warm milk-butter mixture. Beat with wooden spoon for about 3 minutes. (This step can be done in a food processor using a plastic blade.)
3. Add remaining flour by hand. The dough will be soft and sticky. Place in an oiled bowl, brush with oil and cover with plastic wrap. Refrigerate several hours or overnight.

4 Turn dough onto generously floured surface. Pat dough to 1/2 inch thickness. Cut with a 2-inch round cutter. Place on ungreased cookie sheet about 1 inch apart. Brush generously with melted butter.

5 Allow rolls to rise at room temperature about 45 minutes to 1 hour. Bake in preheated 400 degree oven for 10 minutes.

Makes 24 rolls.

BREAD BREAKING — IT NOURISHES THE BODY, SOUL AND SPIRIT!

NOTE:

STORE IN A TIGHTLY

CLOSED CONTAINER AND

USE FOR GARNISHING

SOUPS AND SALADS. IT'S

ALSO A TASTY SNACK.

croutons

We mix these savory croutons into our Caesar Salad in the Tea Room. Ours is a mix of all the breads we bake daily which I think makes a more interesting flavor and texture. Go ahead and mix your own different leftover breads together. The addition of the herb mixture gives unity and binds the flavors.

1/4 cup garlic, minced
1/4 cup onion powder
1/4 cup dried basil
1/4 cup dried oregano
2 tablespoons dried thyme leaves
2 tablespoons dried marjoram leaves
1/4 cup paprika
1/2 cup olive oil
1/2 cup butter, melted
6 cups bread, cut into 1/2-inch cubes, lightly browned

1 Mix dry seasoning ingredients.
2 Stir oil, butter, and dry seasoning together until well mixed.
3 In a large bowl toss browned croutons with oil/seasoning mixture until well coated.
4 Bake at 350 degrees for 20 to 25 minutes - stirring once or twice.

Makes 6 cups.

sandwiches

tea sandwich ideas

BLUE CHEESE, SMOKED TURKEY SLICES, CRANBERRY SALSA. Leave it open faced so you can show all the color of the cranberry salsa.

BUTTER, THEN BROWN SUGAR spread on slices of thin bread — best if made a couple of hours before serving so the brown sugar gets soft and caramelly.

FRESH HERB SPREAD on thin slices of buttered bread - if served open faced a tiny violet blossom or johnny jump-up is pretty.

THIN SLICES OF RED ONION AND CUCUMBERS on thin slices of buttered bread and lightened mayonnaise. If done open- faced add a sprinkle of flower confetti.

ASPARAGUS SPEARS (cooked until crisp tender!) on soft white bread, crusts removed, spread with homemade mayonnaise . I first learned to make these when we moved to Fredericksburg 30 years ago at one of Roberta Warren's garden luncheons. As a young wife and mother just beginning to think about entertaining myself, I was inspired by watching how easily and gracefully Roberta managed to entertain her guests.

PEANUT BUTTER AND JAM I've done these for wedding receptions for the children — I've learned to do extra for the "much older" children!

BLUE CHEESE SPREAD on thin slices of bread with crisp bacon.

FINELY CHOPPED SWEET ONION on thin slices of buttered bread, basic mayonnaise and — a basil leaf adds a pretty and tasty accent!

SEAFOOD SALAD SANDWICHES - Seafood Sandwich Spread (see this section) on buttered bread. Garnish open faced sandwiches with capers or a flower.

TINY BLT - buttered bread, mayonnaise, 1 or 2 thin slices of cherry tomato, and crumbled crispy bacon on top.

WHEN MAKING TEA SANDWICHES WITH FILLINGS THAT CONTAIN MAYONNAISE - BUTTER THE BREAD SLICES LIGHTLY TO PREVENT A SOGGY SANDWICH.

IN THE TEA ROOM WE
USE ROASTED GARLIC
MAYONNAISE;
HOWEVER, ANY GOOD
QUALITY MAYONNAISE
IS FINE.

DURING THE SEASON,
USE HOME GROWN
TOMATOES — OFF
SEASON, USE OVEN
ROASTED TOMATOES
TO BRING OUT THE
TOMATO FLAVOR.

southwest BLT

Canadian bacon in this sandwich is very good — and lean!

4 slices Jalapeño Potato Garlic Bread (see Breads)
2 tablespoons Roasted Garlic Mayonnaise (see this section)
4 slices Canadian bacon
4 to 6 slices homegrown tomatoes
Generous handful - dark green lettuce or red tipped lettuce

Spread bread with mayonnaise. Layer bacon, tomatoes and lettuce onto bread; top with second slice.

Makes 2 sandwiches.

fried green tomato BLT

This is a really great twist on the favorite BLT that is such a classic. Be sure to fry extra tomatoes for snacking!

4 slices Rosemary Roasted Garlic Potato Bread (see Breads)
2 tablespoons Roasted Red Pepper Garlic Mayonnaise
(see this section)
6 to 8 slices Fried Green Tomatoes (see Side Dishes)
6 to 8 slices bacon, crisp
Dark green lettuce leaves or red tip lettuce

Spread bread with mayonnaise. Layer rest of ingredients; top with second slice.

Makes 2 sandwiches.

hot ham or turkey sandwich

One of the giant blessings we have received from our son's marriage to Helana is getting to spend time with her precious family. I always come away from Lynda Beal's home with a new food experience to savor! I still remember the wonderful time we spent at their ranch home, sitting around her table to enjoy these delicious sandwiches. They can be assembled the day before — wrapped in foil — then placed in the oven just before lunchtime to heat, making it possible to enjoy those special moments with family!

4 Kaiser rolls or onion buns
I/2 cup butter softened
2 tablespoons mustard
2 tablespoons poppy seeds
4 slices of ham or turkey
4 slices of Swiss cheese

1 Preheat oven to 300 degrees.
2 Cream together butter, mustard and poppy seeds.
3 Spread on both sides of buns. Layer turkey or ham with Swiss cheese. Top with bun.
4 Wrap in foil and heat for 30 minutes. Or heat in microwave for 30 seconds (plastic wrap instead of foil). These can be assembled, and frozen individually to have on hand for quick lunches.

Makes 4 sandwiches.

NOTE:

LYNDA SOMETIMES MAKES UP THE BUTTER MIXTURE TO KEEP IN HER REFRIGERATOR — IT KEEPS INDEFINITELY. IT'S AN EASY AND FAST LUNCH — GREAT SERVED WITH A FRESH FRUIT SALAD!

green olives

♡ NOTES:

SOME SUGGESTIONS FOR

MEATS AND CHEESES ARE

PROVOLONE,

MOZZARELLA, GENOA

SALAMI, MORTADELLA

AND CAPICOLA.

THE SPREAD ITSELF WILL

KEEP IN THE REFRIGERA-

TOR FOR ONE WEEK.

new muffulata sandwich

There are many different ways to make a muffulata sandwich (and many different ways to spell it). This is the one that has become such a favorite in our Tea Room. It is best if made one or two hours before serving so the flavors can marry, which makes it a very nice choice for picnics, or supper in the garden. Men especially are pleased when I serve it at parties.

2 cups pimento
2 cups canned artichokes
1-1/2 cups green olives, pitted
1 cup Kalamata olives, pitted
2 cups parsley
2-1/2 cups Parmesan cheese, grated
1/4 cup olive oil
1 loaf Peach Tree Country French Bread or home style
French bread (see Breads)

❶ Place first 5 ingredients in food processor. Pulse until coarsely chopped. For a finer texture pulse 2 to 3 times more.
❷ Fold in Parmesan cheese and olive oil.
❸ Cut bread in half lengthwise. Remove some bread from the center of the loaf to make more room for spread. Apply 1/4 to 1/2 inch spread to both halves. Layer meats and cheeses of your choice.
❹ Can be served immediately or wrap sandwiches in plastic wrap and refrigerate for several hours until serving. Slice in 2-inch wedges and serve.

Makes 4 cups.

black olives

130

seafood sandwich spread

If you have my first cookbook, **The Peach Tree Tea Room Cookbook**, you will know what an influence my Aunt Jo had on my love of cooking. When I visited her and my grandmother in Michigan I was exposed to a world much different from that of the Texas Hill Country I called home. These seafood sandwiches are part of my memories. They were served to friends in my grandmother's lovely gardens one summer during my visit. If served in the spring or early summer a violet or johnny jump-up garnish is very romantic looking.

3/4 cup celery
1/2 cup red onion
3/4 cup cooked shelled shrimp
1/2 cup cooked crab
1/4 cup red pepper, finely chopped
1/2 cup mayonnaise
Dash of Worcestershire sauce
Garnish: capers

❶ Finely chop first five ingredients.
❷ Toss together with mayonnaise and Worcestershire sauce, mixing well.

Makes 3 cups.

SPREAD FILLING ON

BUTTERED, THINLY

SLICED BREAD. PRETTY

SERVED AS OPEN

FACED SANDWICHES

DECORATED WITH VIOLET

OR CHIVE BLOSSOMS.

BUTTERING THE BREAD

KEEPS THE SANDWICHES

FROM BECOMING SOGGY.

herb sandwich filling

I consider this recipe one of the prize entries in this book. When I think "picnic" for myself, these sandwiches must be included. The flavors are an expression of the very essence of spring. I first enjoyed herb sandwiches while visiting my grandmother's home in Birmingham, Michigan. When my Aunt Jo told me how to make them for myself, she emphasized that the key ingredient is fresh basil along with homemade mayonnaise. The other herbs and the amounts used can vary a little, but I agree that fresh basil is a must!

1/2 cup onion, quartered
4 cups parsley
I cup fresh basil
2 tablespoons fresh oregano
4 tablespoons lemon balm
2 tablespoons fresh dill (or 2 teaspoons dried dill)
I teaspoon Worcestershire sauce
1/3 cup Basic Mayonnaise (see this section) or good quality processed mayonaisse
Salt to taste

❶ In small amounts, place onions and herbs in bowl of food processor to chop very finely.
❷ Add Worcestershire sauce, mayonnaise and mix well until herbs are well moistened.

Makes I cup.

My potted herb garden

NOTE:

To make a roasted

green chile spread —

just omit the

jalapeños and add

roasted green chilies

to taste!

jalapeño-pimento cheese spread

Even though this recipe appeared in the **Peach Tree Family Cookbook**, I wanted to include it here. Served on the Super Good for You Bread, it is one of our favorite sandwiches in the Tea Room. And whenever we send out tea sandwiches these are requested in the assortment. It is also in one of the Salad Sandwich Cake ingredients, and I just didn't want you to miss out on something so good! Enjoy!

3 cups grated Cheddar cheese
1-1/2 cups grated Monterey Jack cheese
1/2 cup chopped pimentos
2 tablespoons chopped pickled jalapeños with juice
1 cup good quality mayonnaise
1 cup Miracle Whip

Combine all ingredients and mix well.

Makes 6 cups.

basic mayonnaise

Just plain good mayonnaise — great on sandwiches, hamburgers and salads, and so very easy to prepare!

2 eggs
I egg yolk
3 tablespoons lemon juice
I tablespoon cider vinegar
I/4 teaspoon cayenne pepper
I teaspoon salt
I/2 teaspoon white pepper
2 cups canola oil

❶ Place all ingredients in food processor - except oil.
❷ Start machine and add oil gradually.

Makes 3 cups.

mayonnaise - lightened

Try this if you want to cut down on fat grams. It may even become your preference!

I/2 cup Basic Mayonnaise
I/2 cup plain non fat yogurt

Mix. Serving size is I tablespoon.

Makes 16 servings.

NOTE:

STIR INTO MAYONAISSE 2-3 TABLESPOONS CHUTNEY AND 2 TEASPOONS CURRY POWDER. SPREAD ON SUPER GOOD FOR YOU BREAD (SEE BREADS) WITH HAM OR TURKEY, LETTUCE, WHITE CHEDDAR AND PINEAPPLE. MAKES AN EXCELLENT SANDWICH!

KEEPS IN THE REFRIGERATOR 4 TO 5 DAYS.

roasted garlic mayonnaise

I like the flavor this gives to the Southwest BLT and our Super
Good for You Sandwich. It also makes the simplest ham and Swiss
cheese sandwich rise to new heights!

I green onion
3 tablespoons parsley
3 eggs
I tablespoon Roasted Garlic (see Side Dishes)
2 tablespoons balsamic vinegar
2 teaspoons Dijon mustard
I teaspoon salt
I teaspoon pepper
2-I/2 cups canola oil

❶ Combine all ingredients except oil in a food processor or
blender. Process until finely chopped and well blended.
❷ With machine running, slowly add oil, allowing the mayonnaise
to thicken as the oil is added.
❸ Cover and refrigerate. It will keep up to five days.

Makes 2-I/4 cups.

orange and roasted garlic mayonnaise

I made this mayonnaise when we created the Holiday Chicken Salad (see this section). The orange is a good complement to the cranberries and onions we use in the recipe. Try it also for pork loin sandwiches.

1 orange, peeled and seeded
2 green onions
3/4 cup cilantro leaves
3 eggs
2 tablespoons Roasted Garlic (see Side Dishes)
2 tablespoons cider vinegar
2 teaspoons dry mustard
1 teaspoon salt
1 teaspoon white pepper
About 3 cups canola oil

1. Combine all ingredients except oil in a food processor or blender. Process until finely chopped and well blended.
2. With machine running, slowly add oil, allowing the mayonnaise to thicken as the oil is added. Keeps in the refrigerator up to 5 days.

Makes 4 cups.

roasted red pepper & garlic mayonnaise

This is the mayonnaise we use on our Fried Green Tomato BLT (see this section). As you can tell — I love the flavor that roasting gives to red peppers. It's a nice extra touch!

1 green onion
3 eggs
2 tablespoons Roasted Garlic (see Sides Dishes)
2 tablespoons balsamic vinegar
1 tablespoon Dijon mustard
1 teaspoon salt
1 teaspoon pepper
1/2 cup Roasted Red Peppers (see Side Dishes)
4 tablespoons fresh parsley
2-1/2 cups canola oil

❶ Combine all ingredients except oil in food processor or blender. Process until finely chopped and well blended.
❷ With machine running, slowly add oil, allowing mayonnaise to thicken as the oil is added.
❸ Cover and refrigerate. It will keep up to 5 days.

Makes 2-1/2 cups.

super good for you sandwich

I look forward to the times we feature this sandwich as a special on our menu. The flavors work so well together — it's really worth the extra effort it will take to bake the bread!

4 slices Super Good for You Bread (see Breads)
2 tablespoons Roasted Garlic Mayonnaise (see this section)
3 fresh spinach leaves (enough to cover sandwich)
4 slices Oven Roasted Tomatoes (see Side Dishes)
1/2 cup gruyere cheese, grated
1 avocado, sliced
3 or 4 thin slices red onion

Spread bread with Roasted Garlic Mayonnaise. Layer with rest of ingredients; top with second slice of bread.

Makes 2 sandwiches.

savory salad sandwich cake

YES, EVERY WORD OF THIS TITLE IS ACCURATE! It's a sandwich filled with salads, frosted with goat cheese or cream cheese so it looks like a cake and is served like a cake! The presentation can be a real show-stopper at parties. Depending on the fillings used it can be substantial for a hearty meal, or light and delicate for a tea or ladies luncheon.

There are lots of ways to do this "cake," depending on the shape and size of the bread you use. For the "sandwich cake" that we pictured, I baked the bread in square pans and sliced the layers horizontally.

Because I wanted a flat top, I sliced away and discarded the pouffy rounded top of the loaf. And also wanting a tall "cake," I baked two loaves of bread so I could have more layers. And for ease of frosting the "cake" I flipped the loaf over so that I had a smooth surface with which to work.

The "sandwich cake" is filled with Italian peasant style fillings — fresh Mozzarella and Sun-Dried Tomato Pesto, Oven Roasted Tomatoes and fresh basil leaves, and chopped hard boiled eggs with Roasted Garlic Mayonnaise and fresh asparagus. For the frosting I used one third part goat cheese with two thirds part cream cheese. I mixed it until smooth, creamy and spreadable in my food processor.

The flower stems are thin asparagus spears with coreopsis flowers, Italian parsley flowers, and sprigs of oregano at the base for the "foundation planting."

I made another "sandwich cake" recently for a young girl's tea party. I filled it with Jalapeño Cheese Spread, cream cheese and olive spread, and Almond Chicken Salad. The frosting was cream cheese and a little bit of milk, mixed in the food processor until creamy and spreadable. For the "garden" I used the light purple blossoms of society garlic, little pink yarrow flowers, along with the ferny yarrow foliage and garlic chives for the flower stems.

The "cake" can also be done in the traditional loaf shape. And, baking your bread in a springform pan gives a nice shape for a round "cake." The number of layers is totally up to you — I like to do three or more fillings because the colors are so pretty when the "cake" is sliced.

When I'm preparing to decorate these "cakes" I wander through my garden for inspiration. I like to look for tiny flowers and greens for the scale of the "cake" because my goal is to create a little garden "growing" all around the sides of the "cake." Johnny jump-ups, violets, miniature roses, dill and parsley flowers are some good choices.

For the base of the "cake" I look for the tiny leaves from winter savory, thyme or oregano plants. They give the look of "foundation planting."

You can have such fun doing these "cakes." Some time I will do one for Easter with a curried egg salad and fresh asparagus and thin slices of ham or smoked salmon. Pale yellow and lilac johnny jump-ups always signify "springtime."

Have fun with the ideas — this will just get you started — there is no end to the possibilities — Be creative!

My mother used to tell me that there is really nothing new under the sun. The Creator has already done it all — and I believe He is pleased when He watches us delight in developing new ways of putting it together with Him!

Things that spring up, Praise the Lord!

side dishes

roasting vegetables

THE METHOD FOR OVEN ROASTING IS BASICALLY THE same for all vegetables. A very high oven temperature is required to lock in the flavors. Vegetables cooked in this manner are most flavorful — the natural sugars are released so that the surface has that lovely and delicious caramelization.

Roasted vegetables are so pretty for large parties. I like to arrange several kinds on platters or baskets — they look like glistening jewels! A combination that I particularly like to do is rows of young carrots, asparagus and long red pepper slices.

I love having leftover roasted vegetables in my refrigerator — there are so many ways to use them! Sometimes I chop them and mix together as a topping for Crostini (see Appetizers) or pasta. And layers on crusty bread with fresh basil leaves or a light spreading of pesto make the most elegant panini (Italian "little" sandwiches).

Also keep in mind what a delicious pizza you can make using the vegetables, fresh mozzarella and dollops of fresh pesto!

Roasting vegetables has become my current favorite way of preparation. Very often when Hector and I come home from a busy workday this is the dish we want for dinner. It's fast and easy — and the reward is a meal intensely flavorful, alive with color. Using this method with heat seals in flavors and nutrients. Sometimes I quickly saute a chicken breast, but if I've had a successful hunt at the store we may have just a beautiful arrangement of 4 or 5 kinds of vegetables.

When I go to the grocery store, my favorite place to linger is the produce section. Maybe it's my way of visiting the garden! I like to gather bunches of greens and colorful peppers — I'm forever on a search for some new variety that I've never seen before — it's like a treasure hunt!!

Springtime is especially fun when I call my friend, Marianne, who has an organic farm in Dripping Springs, Texas. She ships boxes of just picked beauties from her gardens by way of the Kerrville Bus line.

Sometimes there are 5 colors of potatoes, multi-colored peppers, Easter egg radishes, fresh leeks, all sizes and colors of eggplants.

This is a spring luxury which can last 3 to 5 months, depending on when the hot summer sun becomes too harsh.

COLORFUL PEPPER BOUQUET!

N O T E :

USE PARCHMENT SHEETS

ON YOUR BAKING PAN. IT

MAKES FOR EASY

CLEANUP!

basic instructions for roasting vegetables

This recipe will give you my basic rules for roasting vegetables. Read ahead to the options that I've listed. I hope that you enjoy using this technique as much as I do!

Vegetable of choice listed on next page
2 to 3 tablespoons olive oil, or more if necessary
Salt to your taste using Kosher salt
1 teaspoon balsamic vinegar

1. Preheat oven to 500 degrees.
2. Spread vegetables of choice in a single layer on a baking sheet. Brush all surfaces of the vegetables with olive oil.
3. Place on the top shelf of your oven and roast until tender (see vegetable roasting times next page). Timing depends on how your oven cooks and depends on the size and thickness of the vegetables.
4. Remove baking sheet from oven, and place vegetables on serving platter. Sprinkle with the salt and balsamic vinegar.
5. Roasted vegetables are delicious served hot from the oven, or set aside and served at room temperature.

vegetables &
cooking times

Please remember that there may be variables for the cooking times due to vegetable quality and thickness and the way your oven cooks!

EGGPLANT: If small ones are used, slice in half lengthwise - if larger, slice into lengthwise slices 1/4 inch thick. Whether to peel or not depends on the quality of the eggplant. Young, tender ones can remain unpeeled. Roast 10 to 12 minutes.

CARROTS: 1 pound small carrots. Scrub (nice to leave 1 inch of the green top on carrots). Roast 10 to 12 minutes.

ZUCCHINI: 1 pound. Cut into flat slices lengthwise 1/4 inch thick. Long diagonal slices are nice too, and if small zucchini are used they can be roasted whole. Roast 8 to 10 minutes.

LEEKS: 1 pound. Slice in half lengthwise. Rinse well, and place cut side up on baking sheet. Roast 10 to 12 minutes.

GREEN ONIONS: 2 or 3 bunches. Small ones are pretty - just trim off any messy leaves and rinse well. Roast 8 to 10 minutes.

BRUSSEL SPROUTS: 1 pound. They roast beautifully - with the little outer leaves turning golden brown. Roast 10 to 12 minutes.

ASPARAGUS: 1 pound. Trim ends, rinse well. Roast 8 to 10 minutes depending on size.

COLORFUL PEPPERS: 1 pound. Red, yellow, orange, green, purple — a mixture of colors can be very pretty! Slice (removing seeds) into 1 inch lengthwise slices. Roast for 8 to 10 minutes until golden.

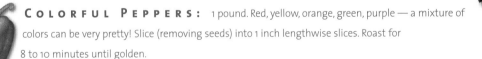

*Use parchment sheets on your baking pan.
It makes for easy clean-up!*

garden fresh garlic

roasted garlic

Roasted garlic can be removed from the skin and kept in the freezer, ready to use in cooking. Roasted garlic has a unique flavor and enhances many recipes, such as Roasted Garlic Mayonnaise. I, myself, never have any left to freeze because we use it in so many ways.

4 to 6 garlic pods
1 tablespoon olive oil
Rosemary sprigs, optional

1. Preheat oven to 350 degrees.
2. Remove loose outer peeling of garlic pods. Slice the tips of each clove so the flesh is exposed.
3. Place on sheet of parchment paper. Drizzle olive oil over top of each garlic pod. Place rosemary with garlic on parchment.
4. Fold parchment around garlic and tuck in ends.
5. Bake for 1 hour. Let cool for 15 minutes before opening parchment.

NOTE:

IN THE TEA ROOM KITCHEN, WE BUY LARGE AMOUNTS OF PEELED GARLIC. BECAUSE MANY OF OUR RECIPES CALL FOR ROASTED GARLIC WE PLACE SEVERAL CUPS OF PEELED GARLIC IN A PAN AND POUR ENOUGH OLIVE OIL OVER TO COVER THE GARLIC. WE ROAST IT IN A 350 DEGREE OVEN UNTIL GOLDEN — ABOUT 30 MINUTES. IT KEEPS WELL IN THE REFRIGERATOR AND THE OLIVE OIL HAS GREAT FLAVOR FOR COOKING!

♡ **NOTE:**

GARLIC SHOULD BE

SLICED, NOT CHOPPED, AS

THE TINY PIECES

CONTAIN MOISTURE AND

TEND TO BURN DURING

THE LENGTH OF TIME THE

POTATOES NEED TO

COOK.

rosemary garlic roasted potatoes

These are the potatoes we serve in the Tea Room for breakfast. I love the intense bite of garlic — so I am generous with it. The potatoes are good and versatile — great with chicken or used on pizza with pesto and fresh Mozzarella cheese! Leftovers can be refrigerated, reheated and used for breakfast tacos!

2 pounds red potatoes, unpeeled, 1-1/2 inch cubes (6-1/2 cups)
5 garlic cloves, sliced lengthwise in half
1/4 cup olive oil
2 tablespoons fresh rosemary leaves, chopped
1 teaspoon Kosher salt
1 teaspoon pepper

1. Preheat oven to 400 degrees.
2. Mix together all ingredients and toss until potatoes are coated.
3. Spread on cookie sheet in single layer.
4. Bake for 25 to 30 minutes.

Makes 8 to 10 cups.

Rosemary-Remembrance

roasted beets

I love the color and flavor that beets add to a platter of roasted vegetables. I learned this very simple and delicious way to prepare them from my friend, Marianne, who grows them every year in her commercial organic garden. Preparing beets this way seals in the flavors and the nutrients.

1 bunch fresh beets, whole, unpeeled
Balsamic vinegar

❶ Place beets in a covered casserole, or wrap them securely in parchment paper. Place in a 375 degree oven and cook until beets are tender or about 45 minutes to 1 hour. The time will vary depending on the size of the beets.

❷ When the beets are tender, remove them from the oven, and peel them under running water - the peelings should slip off easily.

❸ Slice and serve. Sprinkle with just a little balsamic vinegar, 1 to 2 teaspoons.

Makes 4 servings.

Pea Pudding for the little people

When David and Helana married they discovered that for both of them green peas is a favorite vegetable. Peas are served often to Claire and Rose who are always pleased. This recipe from my friend, Charles Schmidt, is delicious and elegant for the most formal dinners. And in my family there are times when we call it pea pudding for the "little people"!

english-pea souffle

1-16 ounce package frozen peas
5 eggs
1/2 cup whipping cream
1 cup finely grated farmer's cheese
1/4 teaspoon nutmeg
1/2 teaspoon salt
1/4 teaspoon white pepper

❶ Preheat oven to 300 degrees.
❷ Butter or spray 6 individual ramekins or custard dishes with non-stick spray. Thaw peas, puree in food processor or blender, adding eggs and cream.
❸ Add cheese and seasonings and blend to a smooth consistency.
❹ Spoon mixture into prepared ramekins, filling 2/3 full. Place souffles in a pan and add water to pan until half-way up the sides of dish. Bake 1 hour. Remove from oven, invert ramekins on serving platter and serve hot.

Makes 6 servings.

NOTE:

TO MAKE 12, MAKE TWO INDIVIDUAL BATCHES RATHER THAN DOUBLING THE RECIPE. THROUGH TRIAL AND ERROR, MANY OF US WHO LOVE TO COOK HAVE FOUND THAT SOME RECIPES CAN BE DOUBLED — AND FOR OTHERS IT JUST DOESN'T WORK WELL. THIS IS ONE TIME YOU WILL NEED TO MAKE IT ONE RECIPE AT A TIME.

oven roasted tomatoes

These are a real treasure to have on hand in your refrigerator. Use them in pastas or sandwiches. The juice is also great as a salad dressing or a flavor enhancer — once you taste it — it will inspire you!

6 Roma tomatoes, sliced in 1/2 inch thick slices
3 tablespoons olive oil
3 to 4 cloves garlic, sliced thinly
1 teaspoon black pepper, freshly ground
2 teaspoons balsamic vinegar

1. Preheat oven to 350 degrees.
2. Place tomatoes in mixing bowl, with remaining ingredients and toss to distribute ingredients.
3. Spread on a baking sheet in a single layer.
4. Place in oven for 15 to 20 minutes until the tomatoes are bubbly and just tender.
5. Remove from oven and let cool.
6. Store in container in the refrigerator - be sure to keep the juices, too.

Makes 24 slices.

NOTE:

FOR AN HERB VARIATION,

STIR 1/2 CUP FINELY

CHOPPED FRESH HERBS

INTO POTATO MIXTURE.

SOME GOOD CHOICES

WOULD BE PARSLEY,

CHIVES, OR GARLIC.

A PASTRY BLENDER

WORKS WELL FOR THIS

SMALL AMOUNT OF

POTATOES.

potato puffs

These potatoes really do puff up when fried and are a nice accompaniment to the Flank Steak (see Entrees). I like to cut them in heart shapes to serve to my little granddaughters, Claire and Rose. They make fun appetizers, too!

I pound red potatoes, peeled and quartered
I to 2 teaspoons salt
1/2 cup all-purpose flour
I quart corn oil

❶ Cook potatoes until very tender, 20 to 30 minutes. Drain well. Mash potatoes. Add salt.

❷ Stir flour into potatoes until smooth. On a lightly floured surface, roll out the dough to a 12-inch round and about 1/4 inch thick using a floured rolling pin. Stamp out 2-1/2 inch rounds with a floured glass or a biscuit cutter. Place on round clean kitchen towel.

❸ Fry potato rounds in hot corn oil. Fry about 1/3 of them at one time, until they are puffed and golden brown. Sprinkle with salt and serve right away.

Makes about 15 puffs.

fried green tomatoes

These are just good eating anytime! Great on sandwiches and as a side dish for summer and fall parties. In a summer buffet, serve them next to a bowl of roasted red peppers and Roasted Garlic Mayonnaise (see Sandwiches) for garnish!

1 cup yellow corn meal
1/4 cup unbleached flour
2 pounds green tomatoes, 1/2 inch slices
2 tablespoons bacon grease
Canola oil, 1/4 inch in pan

❶ Coat tomato slices with cornmeal-flour mixture.
❷ Fry in hot bacon grease-oil mixture until golden. Drain on paper towel.

Makes 4 generous servings.

poblano corn pudding

For me going to Santa Fe means that I'm going to eat at Pasqual's!
It's one of my all time favorite restaurants — anywhere. I asked
for this recipe several years ago and was so happy when I received it
in the mail after returning home. It is called a pudding, but it is
baked in a bundt pan — looking regal before it is sliced into wedges
for serving. Serve this as a side dish and your simplest meal will
become a feast to remember!

1 poblano chile, roasted, peeled, seeded and diced
3 cups corn kernels
1 cup butter
1/2 cup brown sugar, packed
1-1/3 teaspoons baking soda
2-1/2 teaspoons baking powder
1-1/3 tablespoons red chile powder
1 tablespoon salt
5 eggs, separated
1 cup milk
2 cups unbleached flour

1. Preheat oven to 350 degrees.
2. Prepare a bundt pan by greasing it well, and set aside.
3. In a small bowl mix together the chile and corn. Set aside.
4. In a large mixing bowl, cream together the butter, sugar, baking soda, baking powder, chile powder, and salt.
5. Separate the eggs, placing the yolks and whites in separate bowls. Beat the egg whites until stiff and set aside.
6. Whip the egg yolks until well blended and add to the creamed mixture. Add milk and flour alternately. With the mixer set on low speed, blend well. Place in large bowl and add chile and corn mixture.
7. By hand, gradually fold in the beaten egg whites.
8. Pour into the prepared bundt pan. Place in the oven and bake for 40 minutes to one hour or until a wooden skewer comes out clean. Remove from the oven and let cool before turning out of the pan.

Makes 12 to 14 servings.

NOTE:

PASQUAL'S ALSO MAKES AN AMAZING CHOCOLATE COOKIE, BUT YOU'LL HAVE TO VISIT THEM IN PERSON IN SANTA FE BECAUSE THAT RECIPE THEY ARE KEEPING FOR THEMSELVES!

Long live the sun which gives us such color!
Cezanne

oven roasted sweet potatoes

I love to eat roasted vegetables, and the more variety I can use at one meal the happier I am! Each one contributes different health benefits and flavors. Serve these potatoes in combination with other vegetables or let them stand alone — they are wonderful!

2 to 3 tablespoons olive oil
3 tablespoons maple syrup
I tablespoon Roasted Garlic, mashed slightly (see this section)
1/2 teaspoon salt or to your taste
I pound sweet potatoes, partially baked, peeled, 1/2 inch slices

❶ Preheat oven to 400 degrees.
❷ In bowl, mix olive oil, maple syrup, garlic and salt. Add sweet potatoes and toss to coat surfaces well.
❸ Spread sweet potatoes in a single layer on a baking sheet.
❹ Place on top shelf of oven and roast until tender and beginning to brown — about 10 to 15 minutes. Serve.

Makes 4 servings.

NOTE:

SWEET POTATOES CAN BE
PARTIALLY BAKED IN THE
OVEN, OR TO SAVE TIME,
IN THE MICROWAVE FOR
2 TO 3 MINUTES.

entrees

NOTE:

THIS IS AN EASY

RECIPE TO ADJUST FOR

APPETIZERS — JUST CUT

THE EGGPLANT SLICES

SMALLER AND ADD

SMALLER AMOUNTS OF

FILLING — THEY ARE

GOOD HOT OR AT ROOM

TEMPERATURE.

eggplant rolatini

I love to eat eggplant! This is one of my favorite dishes to use when I cater parties — it's colorful and delicious! It's also great as a side dish with Chicken Milanesa, salad and, of course, a loaf of crusty bread.

1 large eggplant, 1 -1/4 or 1 -1/2 pounds
Salt
Olive oil

Filling:
4 cloves garlic
1 cup parsley, loosely packed
1 -1/2 cups bread crumbs
1 -3/4 cups Mozzarella cheese, grated
3 eggs
1 teaspoon pepper, freshly ground
1/2 teaspoon salt
2 cups Tomato Basil Marinara (see this section)
3/4 cup Parmesan cheese, grated

1. Slice eggplant lengthwise into 1/4 inch slices - 12 to 14 slices depending on size and shape of eggplant. Lightly sprinkle slices with salt - layer in bowl and let stand about 30 minutes to release water - press slices between paper towels to blot out moisture.

2. Place on baking sheet - brush both sides with olive oil. Roast at 400 degrees until done, 8 to 10 minutes.

3. In food processor, place garlic, parsley and bread crumbs. Process until garlic and parsley are well chopped. Add remaining ingredients (except Parmesan and Marinara)- process until incorporated - do not over process.

4. Place 2 heaping tablespoons of filling on the end of each roasted eggplant strip. Roll up and place seam side down in baking pan. Pour Marinara over the Rollatini and sprinkle with Parmesan.

5. Bake for 20 to 25 minutes at 350 degrees. Serve immediately or at room temperature.

Makes 12 to 14

NOTE:

TO PEEL OR NOT TO PEEL? SO MUCH DEPENDS ON THE QUALITY OF THE EGGPLANTS — YOUNGER AND SMALLER EGGPLANTS CAN REMAIN UNPEELED, BUT A MORE MATURE ONE CAN BE PARTIALLY OR COMPLETELY PEELED!

eggplant -delicious and beautiful!

I have used the

oven ready lasagna

noodles for this.

However, because

there's not an excess

of moisture in this

recipe, I soak them in

hot water for 2 to

3 minutes before

assembling the

lasagna.

roasted vegetable lasagna

My love for roasted vegetables led me to create this new lasagna.
It's very colorful, and even more so if you can find yellow tomatoes
for the marinara.

1 8-ounce package oven ready lasagna noodles
1 recipe Bechamel Sauce (recipe follows)
1-1/4 pounds roasted zucchini
1-1/4 pounds roasted eggplant
2 roasted red peppers, peeled
3/4 pound Mozzarella, sliced or grated
1/2 pound fresh Parmesan, grated
2 cups Tomato Basil Marinara (recipe follows)

❶ Preheat oven to 350 degrees.
❷ Cook noodles according to package directions.

Assembly:
❶ Coat 9 x 13 inch casserole dish with non-stick spray.
❷ Pour in 1/4 cup Bechamel Sauce.
❸ Add one layer lasagna noodles.
❹ Pour on 1/2 cup Bechamel Sauce and layer half
   of roasted vegetables.
❺ Layer half of the amount of Parmesan and Mozzarella.
❻ Add another layer of noodles.
❼ Pour on remaining Bechamel Sauce and layer rest
   of roasted vegetables.
❽ Top with Tomato Basil Marinara Sauce.
❾ Sprinkle on rest of Mozzarella and Parmesan cheeses
   and bake for 1 hour.

Makes 10 servings.

Like Glistening Jewels in my kitchen!

ROASTED ZUCCHINI, SQUASH, ASPARAGUS AND RED PEPPERS

OTE:

SEE PREVIOUS RECIPE

FOR INSTRUCTIONS ON

MAKING VEGETABLE

LASAGNA.

bechamel sauce

This is the cream sauce that I use for the vegetable lasagna — it's a good basic and has many other uses. It can be prepared the day before you are to use it and reheated slowly.

8 tablespoons butter
4 tablespoons unbleached flour
2 cups hot milk
2 teaspoons salt
I/4 teaspoon cayenne pepper (optional)
I/2 teaspoon nutmeg, grated (optional)

❶ In a sauce pan, melt butter over low heat. Add flour and stir with a wooden spoon until smooth. Cook for I minute, being careful not to burn the flour.
❷ Remove from heat and slowly add the hot milk, whisking until smooth.
❸ Place on the stove and continue cooking until the sauce is thickened, whisking often. Cook for about 5 minutes so that the sauce will not have a raw flour taste.
❹ Remove from heat, add salt and optional pepper and nutmeg.
❺ Place sauce in bowl and cover surface with waxed paper or plastic wrap, let cool until you are ready to use.

Makes 2 cups.

tomato basil marinara

- sweet basil

I use this sauce to top the Eggplant Rolatini and the Roasted Vegetable Lasagna (both in this section). Make with yellow canned tomatoes if you can find them. I use a brand called D'Oro Yellow Tomatoes. Grown in Texas, they are available in specialty food stores. Very colorful!

4 cloves garlic, sliced lengthwise
2 tablespoons olive oil
I 28-ounce can tomatoes, coarsely chopped
(use fresh tomatoes if desired)
4 tablespoons fresh basil leaves, coarsely chopped
I to 2 teaspoons salt
I teaspoon black pepper, freshly ground
2 teaspoons sugar

❶ Saute garlic in oil, being careful not to burn.
❷ Add tomatoes and simmer for 15 to 20 minutes.
❸ Add basil, salt, pepper and sugar. Simmer 5 minutes.

Makes 3 1/2 cups

The New Chef in the family

My son, David, and I have a memory of going to Washington, D.C. with my mother while David was still in college. The three of us were there for five days, sightseeing, eating good food, and just enjoying being together.

Just last winter, David called me from his home in Boston to talk through his plans to recreate the delicious Salmon Pasta that he enjoyed at an Italian restaurant in Georgetown.

I'm so very proud of his recipe! He made it for all of us when we were together for our family portrait this spring, and it's wonderful.

The flavors are simple, clean and straight forward. It's a really good dish for entertaining — the caviar adds a lovely touch of flavor and elegance.

david's salmon pasta

1 pound salmon filet
1 lemon, sliced
2 teaspoons capers, optional
9 ounces fresh fettuccini
2 cups heavy cream
1 1/2 cups frozen peas
4 tablespoons large red caviar
1 teaspoon salt

1. Preheat oven to 375 degrees.
2. Place salmon on a sheet of aluminum foil or kitchen parchment. Cover with lemon slices and capers. Seal and bake for 20 minutes. Remove from oven and discard lemon and capers. Cut salmon into 1-inch cubes, set aside.
3. Cook fettuccini according to package instructions, drain and set aside.
4. Pour cream into a large skillet and heat until boiling and continue cooking until it is reduced by one third.
5. Add fettuccini, peas and salt to reduced cream, tossing to coat well, add salmon and gently toss to distribute into pasta.
6. Serve at once, garnishing with a dollop of large red caviar and fresh grated Parmesan.

Makes 4 servings.

To Sandra & Bob, with love

lemon penne
pasta with salmon

NOTES:

IF YOU CANNOT FIND

LEMON PEPPER

FLAVORED PASTA, USE

THE PLAIN PENNE PASTA

AND ADD THE ZEST OF

1 LEMON AND 1 TABLE-

SPOON LEMON JUICE

WITH THE TOMATOES.

TWO OF OUR

DEAR FRIENDS AND

CUSTOMERS AT THE

TEA ROOM ARE SANDRA

AND BOB REYNOLDS.

THEY OFTEN REQUEST

THIS TO BE ON OUR

LUNCH MENU.

There are some really good flavored pastas available now. Lemon pepper penne pasta was the beginning inspiration for this delicious dish. We always get raves in the Tea Room when it is the featured special. It's a nice light tasting dish and the appearance is colorful featuring the bright green asparagus and pink salmon. Add a tossed green salad, good bread and a chilled white wine. Feast!!

2 to 3 tablespoons olive oil
2 cups chicken broth
1 cup Oven Roasted Tomatoes (see Side Dishes)
1/3 cup fresh dill, chopped coarsely
1 pound fresh asparagus, cut into 2 inch lengths
12 ounces salmon, cut into 2 inch cubes
6 cups cooked pasta, al dente, (lemon pepper penne pasta)
Garnish: Parmesan, freshly grated and fresh herb sprig

❶ In a large saute pan, add olive oil and chicken broth. Bring to a boil and cook for 2 to 3 minutes to reduce slightly.
❷ Add tomatoes and dill to the pan and simmer for 1 minute.
❸ Add asparagus and salmon and continue to cook for 2 to 3 minutes. Add the pasta to the pan. Stir well to distribute ingredients into pasta and continue heating until pasta is hot.

Serves 4 to 6.

PREPARING THE SALMON PASTA

asparagus in fillo pastry

I don't think I could write a cookbook without another recipe
using fillo pastry! I love the contrast of the paper thin golden
crust wrapped around a tender yummy center. This is a delicious
dish to serve with any grilled entree, and is just as nice as the main
attraction. The salmon variation becomes a perfect spring entree
as well and is beautiful!

2 cups leeks, sliced
1/4 cup butter
1 pound asparagus
1/2 pound Swiss cheese, shredded
1/2 cup slivered almonds
3 eggs
3 tablespoons parsley, chopped
3 tablespoons fresh dill, chopped
1 teaspoon salt
1 teaspoon black pepper, freshly ground
1 red pepper, thinly sliced
2 tablespoons mint, chopped (optional)
2 to 3 tablespoons lemon juice
16 sheets fillo pastry
1/2 cup butter, melted

NOTE:

THIS IS A NICE DISH IF

YOU'RE ENTERTAINING.

YOU CAN MAKE THE

STRUDELS A DAY BEFORE

YOU ARE TO SERVE THEM.

COVER COMPLETELY WITH

PLASTIC WRAP AND KEEP

IN REFRIGERATOR UNTIL

READY TO BAKE.

1. Saute leeks in butter. Add asparagus and saute quickly just until tender.
2. Add remaining ingredients, except fillo and melted butter.
3. Lay out 1 sheet of fillo pastry and brush with melted butter. Place another sheet of fillo on top of the first and brush with butter.
4. Spoon 2/3 cup of asparagus filling along one end of the rectangle, leaving a margin of 2 inches from the end as well as both sides. Fold in both ends and loosely roll up the strudel. Brush with butter and place on a greased baking sheet. Repeat this process until all filling is used.
5. Bake in a preheated 400 degree oven for 35 minutes, or until crust is golden brown. Garnish with a dollop of sour cream. Each strudel serves one person.

Makes 8 servings.

NOTES:

ADD 1/4 CUP SLICED, FRESH, UNCOOKED SALMON FILETS TO FILLING AS YOU ROLL EACH FILLO ROLL.

ADD ROASTED TOMATOES, SLICED CHICKEN, OR SHRIMP.

roasted asparagus &
leek lasagna

Peggy Cox and I have spent many wonderful hours together sharing our love of preparing and enjoying good food. This is her delicious recipe. It's so good served as the vegetable to accompany a grilled meat entree. I like to make it the main attraction of my meal adding a fresh green salad and a crusty loaf of bread. Hector and I discovered, to our delight, how good this dish tastes when served cold or at room temperature. Think of it for a very elegant picnic!

4 pounds asparagus, trimmed
6 tablespoons extra-virgin olive oil, divided use
Salt to taste
4 cups leeks, sliced
1/2 cup unsalted butter, melted
1/2 cup all-purpose flour
2-1/4 cups chicken broth
3/4 cup water
10 ounces mild goat cheese
2 teaspoons lemon zest
1 8-ounce package oven ready lasagna noodles
2 cups Parmesan, freshly grated
1 cup heavy cream

❶ Cut tips off asparagus spears and set aside. Cut remaining stalks into one inch pieces and place on baking sheet. Toss with 4 tablespoons olive oil, coating well.

❷ Roast in a 500 degree preheated oven for 5 to 10 minutes. Shake pan every few minutes. Roast until crisp-tender. Sprinkle the asparagus with salt to taste and let cool.

❸ Saute leeks in 2 tablespoons olive oil until tender. Set aside.

❹ Blend melted butter with flour, stirring constantly for 3 minutes over moderately low heat. With wire whisk gradually blend in broth and water. Simmer for 5 minutes. Add goat cheese, zest and salt to taste while whisking until sauce is smooth.

❺ In 9 x 13-inch baking dish, arrange half of the noodles and spread it with 1/4 of the sauce. Top the sauce with 1/3 roasted asparagus and 1/3 leeks and sprinkle with 1/3 of Parmesan.

❻ Continue to layer pasta, sauce, asparagus, leeks and Parmesan in the same manner, ending with noodles.

❼ In a bowl beat the cream with a pinch of salt until it holds soft peaks.

❽ Arrange reserved asparagus tips decoratively on the noodles and spread the cream over noodles and asparagus tips. Sprinkle the remaining 1/3 cup Parmesan on top.

❾ Bake lasagna in preheated 400 degree oven for 20 to 30 minutes, or until it is golden and bubbling, and let it stand for 10 minutes before serving.

Makes 16 servings.

NOTE:

CAN BE MADE A DAY

AHEAD AND THEN

REFRIGERATED UNBAKED.

eggplant parmesan

This is a dish I developed to serve in the Tea Room when we were open in the evening. I would lift out a portion, place it in an oven proof serving bowl — pour marinara over it, sprinkle generously with fresh grated Parmesan cheese and heat until bubbly. It is a great dish for entertaining and a presentation of which I'm still very proud!

2 large eggplants, peeled and sliced 1/2 inch crosswise
I teaspoon salt
I cup cornmeal
I cup flour
I teaspoon pepper
1-1/2 tablespoons paprika
I cup milk
2 eggs
1/2 pound Italian sausage (optional)
10 slices Mozzarella
10 slices Provolone
I cup Parmesan, freshly grated
Olive oil/canola oil, half of each to fill 1/4 inch in pan
   I recipe Tomato Basil Marinara (see this section)

176

1. Place eggplant slices in colander and sprinkle with salt. Let set about 30 minutes. Drain on paper towels and pat dry.
2. Mix cornmeal, flour, salt, pepper and paprika.
3. In separate bowl, mix milk and eggs. Dip eggplant slices into egg-milk mixture and coat with dry ingredients.
4. Fry eggplant in a combination of oils until golden. Set aside.
5. Remove Italian sausage from casing. Brown and mix with Tomato Basil Marinara.
6. Assemble in 9 x13-inch pan. Spoon 1/3 Tomato Basil Marinara in pan. Place eggplant rounds in sauce. On each eggplant, place a slice Mozzarella, a slice eggplant, a slice Provolone and top with eggplant. Cover with remaining sauce and sprinkle with Parmesan.
7. Bake at 350 degrees for 30 to 45 minutes or until warm.

Makes 8 to 10 servings.

NOTE:

ADD SLICES OF ROSEMARY ROASTED CHICKEN (SEE THIS SECTION) WHEN LAYERING THE INGREDIENTS. IT MAKES THIS DISH EVEN MORE WONDERFUL.

Let your style and imagination guide you!

NOTE:

SERVE THIS WITH A

GREEN SALAD, CRUSTY

BREAD AND A CHILLED

LIGHT WHITE WINE —

YOU WILL FEAST!

shrimp and crab supreme

Good recipes have a life of their own — they go from family to family with some additions here or there. This recipe flowed through Mary Rae Dwyer's family who shared it with others. My good friend, Peggy, said she woke up during the night wanting more of it. Oh, yes, it's that good! Go ahead, splurge with the purchase of crabmeat. You won't regret it!

1/2 onion, sliced
1 bay leaf
3 peppercorns
1 can beer or 3 cups water
2 pounds medium size raw shrimp in shells
6 tablespoons butter, divided use
1/2 onion, chopped
2 cloves garlic, finely chopped
1 medium red bell pepper, thinly sliced
1/4 cup flour
1 cup half and half
1 cup chicken broth
6 ounces thin spaghetti, cooked according to directions, drained
1 package frozen spinach, chopped and drained
1 tablespoon Worcestershire
1 teaspoon Tabasco sauce
1/2 teaspoon nutmeg
1/4 cup dry sherry
1 tablespoon lemon juice (more if desired)
1/2 teaspoon salt
1/2 teaspoon black pepper, freshly ground
1/2 teaspoon garlic salt
1 pint lump crabmeat
1-1/2 cups Parmesan cheese, grated

❶ Combine sliced onion, bay leaves, peppercorns and beer in a deep pot and bring to a boil. Add shrimp and boil 5 minutes. Drain, let cool and shell. Set aside.

❷ Melt 2 tablespoons butter and saute chopped onion, garlic and red bell pepper until wilted. Set aside.

❸ Melt remaining butter, add flour gradually and then add half and half to make a thick cream sauce. Thin with chicken stock until the consistency of syrup.

❹ In a large container mix spaghetti, spinach, chopped onion and red bell pepper. Pour cream mixture over all and mix well.

❺ Combine crabmeat and shrimp mixture. Add Worcestershire, Tabasco, nutmeg, sherry, lemon juice, salt, pepper and garlic salt.

❻ Place all in a well greased 13 x 9-inch casserole. Sprinkle with grated cheese.

❼ Bake in 350 degree oven for 45 minutes to 1 hour.

Makes 8 to 10.

Hector and I began our life together in Puerto Rico. In his Mustang convertible we would drive to a little seaside 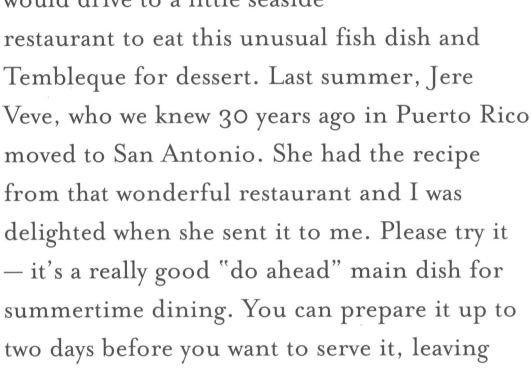 restaurant to eat this unusual fish dish and Tembleque for dessert. Last summer, Jere Veve, who we knew 30 years ago in Puerto Rico moved to San Antonio. She had the recipe from that wonderful restaurant and I was delighted when she sent it to me. Please try it — it's a really good "do ahead" main dish for summertime dining. You can prepare it up to two days before you want to serve it, leaving yourself plenty of time for other activities such as making a fresh flower arrangement or taking a nap!!

pescado en escabeche (pickled fish)

Sauce:

1 cup olive oil
1 cup canola oil
1 cup vinegar
12 peppercorns
1/2 teaspoon salt
2 bay leaves
1-1/2 pounds onions, peeled and sliced

Mix ingredients in a large kettle and cook slowly for 1 hour. Cool.

3 pounds firm fleshed fish fillets, cut into 1 inch slices
Juice of 1 large lime
4-1/2 teaspoons salt
1/4 cup flour
1 cup canola oil
2 large cloves garlic, peeled and crushed

❶ Rinse fish under running water and pat dry. Sprinkle lime juice over fish slices and season with salt.
❷ Flour both sides of the fish slices lightly when ready to fry.
❸ Heat canola oil with garlic. Remove garlic when it's browned.
❹ Brown fish on both sides in canola oil over moderate heat.
❺ Cook until done.
❻ In a deep glass dish layer fish and sauce, beginning with fish.
❼ Cover and put in refrigerator for at least 24 hours before serving. Serve cold.

Makes 6 to 8 servings.

NOTE:

I PREFER TO USE FISH SUCH AS ORANGE ROUGHY, HALIBUT OR COD

sherried shrimp

Over the years, there are recipes I've collected and used often that have been shared with me and which I have really enjoyed. This one from Jane Cummings is very special. If you have any left over, it's a good snack served cold the next day.

1/2 cup dry sherry
1/2 cup orange juice
1 roasted red pepper, cut into strips
1 can ripe olives, pitted
4 tablespoons parsley, chopped
5 cloves garlic, minced
2 teaspoons capers (optional)
3/4 can tomato paste (small can)
1 teaspoon sugar
1 teaspoon black pepper, freshly ground
2 pounds fresh shrimp, peeled
2 teaspoons olive oil
Salt to taste
6 ounces angel hair pasta, cooked according to package directions

❶ Combine sherry, orange juice, red pepper strips, olives, parsley, garlic, capers, tomato paste, sugar and black pepper. Bring to boil.
❷ Add shrimp. Cook and stir about 3 minutes or until shrimp is done. Remove from heat.
❸ Stir in olive oil and salt to taste. Add more olive oil if needed. If too dry, add more sherry.
❹ Serve over angel hair pasta in bowls.

Makes 4 to 6 servings.

pumpkin seed crusted
rainbow trout

There was a time when we opened the Tea Room for evening dining. The Tea Room looked country elegant and we called it "Peach Tree After Hours." This was one of the favorite dishes we served. It is very simple and always a big hit with everyone!

3/4 cup walnuts
1/3 cup sunflower seeds
1/4 cup pumpkin seeds, toasted
1/3 cup Peach Tree Blackened Seasoning (see this section)
1/3 cup unbleached flour
2 tablespoons white cornmeal
2 eggs
3/4 cup milk
4 trout about 10 inches long
Canola oil for frying - 1/4 to 1/2 inch deep in skillet

❶ In food processor place walnuts, sunflower seeds, pumpkin seeds, Blackened Seasoning, flour and cornmeal and pulse until nuts are finely chopped. Place in bowl.

❷ In a separate shallow bowl, mix together egg and milk.

❸ Dip trout into egg-milk mixture and then into seasoning-flour mixture.

❹ Heat oil in large skillet.

❺ Fry fish one at a time in hot oil, turning once or twice until golden and crispy on both sides. Remove from hot oil and drain on paper towels, and repeat with other fish until all are done. Serve at once.

Makes 4 servings.

NOTE:

I LIKE TO BAKE AND

SERVE THIS POT PIE

IN MY HEART SHAPED

PAN — CAN ALSO BE

BAKED IN A 9 X 13-INCH

GLASS BAKING DISH

chicken pot pie with herb crust

"Nothin' says lovin'" and home better than chicken pot pie! This recipe makes a dish that is pure comfort. It's oh, so good — all dressed up with tender chunks of chicken, fresh veggies, tasty thickened broth and pretty flaky herbed crust.

Filling:
2 cups sliced leeks
1 cup carrots, sliced 1 inch
1 cup celery, sliced diagonally 1 inch
8 to 12 mushrooms, quartered if large, otherwise leave whole so you have a nice texture
1/4 cup butter
2 cups chicken breast, cooked, cut into 2 inch cubes

❶ In small skillet, saute leeks, carrots, celery and mushrooms in butter until tender. Remove vegetables and place in baking dish leaving as much butter as possible in the pan.
❷ Add chicken to baking dish.

Sauce:
2 tablespoons butter
1/2 cup flour
3 cups broth
2 cups milk
1 teaspoon black pepper, freshly ground
1 teaspoon salt

Poultry is for me cook what canvas is for me painter.

184

❶ Melt butter in the same saucepan and add flour, stirring until smooth and thickened.

❷ Add broth, milk, salt and pepper. Stir or whisk, until thickened.

❸ Pour over the vegetables and chicken in the baking dish.

Crust:

3 cups unbleached flour, unsifted
1 teaspoon salt
1/2 cup parsley, finely chopped, loosely packed
1/4 cup green onions
1 tablespoon dried dill
4 tablespoons Crisco shortening
12 tablespoons chilled butter (not margarine)
10 tablespoons iced water

❶ Mix flour, salt, parsley, onions and dill in bowl. Cut in Crisco and butter with a pastry blender until crumbly and resembles large curd cottage cheese.

❷ Add iced water, a little at a time, mixing with a fork until well blended. Place dough into plastic bag and gently press dough together into a flat disk. Refrigerate dough for 30 to 60 minutes.

❸ Roll out Herb Crust to fit the shape of the pan. Place over the chicken and vegetables - crimping the sides. Make slashes in top to let air escape while baking.

❹ Bake in a preheated 400 degree oven for 30 to 40 minutes.

Makes 1 large single pot pie or 6 to 8 small individual pot pies

NOTE:

I PLACE THE CHICKEN

BREASTS BETWEEN

2 SHEETS OF PLASTIC

FOOD WRAP, OR INSERT

IN ZIP LOCK BAG,

THEN POUND WITH

MEAT TENDERIZER —

THE PLASTIC PREVENTS

SPATTERS.

chicken breast milanesa

This is a really delicious way to prepare chicken. My friend, Sue Bellows, introduced me to a technique she discovered during her "living in Italy for a summer" period. The taste is magnifico and her experience of living in Italy is one that I covet to this day! The chicken can be served immediately after it is cooked with Tomato Basil Marinara — or — best of all — alfresco (room temperature) garnished with fresh lemon slices. The French Lentil Salad (see Salads) is a nice accompaniment.

2 cups fresh bread crumbs
2 to 3 cloves garlic
2 teaspoons paprika
1 teaspoon salt
2 tablespoons fresh parsley (preferably Italian flat leaf)
1/3 cup Parmesan cheese
10 chicken breasts, skinless and boneless, pounded flat
3 to 4 egg whites
Canola oil and olive oil , half of each to 1/2 inch in skillet

❶ Place bread crumbs, garlic, paprika, salt, parsley and Parmesan cheese together in a food processor and process until you have a fine crumbly mixture.

❷ Dip chicken breasts in egg whites and coat in bread crumb mixture. Place on cookie sheet and refrigerate at least 1 hour (or overnight).

❸ Pour equal amounts of canola oil and olive oil - to fill 1/2 inch in skillet. Saute the chicken breasts in hot oils and place on paper towels to drain.

❹ Arrange on platter with garnish of lemon slices. Serve hot or at room temperature.

Makes 10 servings.

rosemary roasted chicken

Chicken roasted with lemon, garlic and rosemary becomes a splendid feast whether you are serving an elegant dinner or an informal picnic. You are twice blessed by enjoying the fragrant aromas while your chicken is roasting.

1 roasting chicken, 4 to 5 pounds
Salt and black pepper, freshly ground
2 to 3 lemons, thinly sliced
8 sprigs tender fresh rosemary
10 cloves garlic, sliced lengthwise
2 to 3 tablespoons butter, melted
Paprika

1. Preheat oven to 450 degrees.
2. Wash chicken thoroughly. Drain and pat dry. Sprinkle cavity and outside of chicken with salt and pepper.
3. Place slices of one lemon, 6 cloves garlic and several sprigs of rosemary in cavity. Carefully place remaining lemon slices, rosemary sprigs and garlic under skin of chicken.
4. Brush with melted butter and sprinkle with paprika.
5. Bake at 400 degrees for 45 minutes to one hour. Reduce heat to 325 degrees and bake for another 45 minutes. Remove from oven and let chicken rest for 20 minutes before serving. May be served warm or at room temperature.

Makes 6 servings.

NOTES:

FOR A "NEW" STUFFED

PEPPER TRY PUTTING

THIS MEAT MIXTURE IN

RED BELL PEPPERS AND

BAKING UNCOVERED AT

375 DEGREES FOR 45

MINUTES TO ONE HOUR.

MY FRIEND, IGA CLARK,

LINES HER MEATLOAF

PAN WITH ROASTED, OR

SLIGHTLY SAUTEED EGG-

PLANT SLICES, PUTS IN

THE MEAT MIXTURE AND

FOLDS THE SLICES OVER

THE TOP TO ENCLOSE, SO

THAT IT LOOKS LIKE A

BASKET WEAVE, THEN

BAKES. I TRIED HER

METHOD AND IT'S REALLY

GOOD. A CREATIVE

TOUCH TO A CLASSIC

RECIPE!

madeleine's meat loaf

This meat loaf has become affectionately known in our Tea Room kitchen as Madeleine's Meat Loaf because Madeleine Stowe orders it often for her family meals. In fact, I really created it just for her. She and I both like that it's light in flavor and texture. Note that it's made with beef and turkey and flavored with green apples and fresh ginger. It's very good served with our Tomato Basil Marinara (see this section) — made with red or yellow tomatoes.

2 to 3 tablespoons ginger, chopped
4 cloves garlic, chopped
1 medium onion, chopped (1-1/2 cup)
1 medium apple, unpeeled, chopped
2 eggs plus 1 egg white
1 cup French bread crumbs or 1 cup oatmeal
1/2 cup milk
1-1/2 pounds ground beef
1-1/2 pounds ground turkey
1 teaspoon black pepper, freshly ground
2 teaspoons salt
2 roasted red peppers, sliced (optional)
8 slices Oven Roasted Tomatoes (see Side Dishes)

❶ Place ginger and garlic in food processor. Pulse until finely chopped. Add onion and apple and pulse until finely chopped.
❷ Mix in eggs, bread crumbs or oatmeal, milk, ground beef and turkey, salt and pepper. Put half the meat mixture into a lightly oiled pan. Layer optional red peppers on meat and top with remaining meat mixture. Top with Oven Roasted Tomatoes. Bake for 1 hour 15 minutes in a preheated 350 degree oven.

Makes 8 to 10 servings.

flank steak with mushrooms and blue cheese

This dish has become a tradition for the Schmidt family —
Charles has used it for entertaining and now his son, Stuart,
serves it as his specialty when he entertains. It is so satisfying
to see our next generation carrying on the family traditions!

1 3-pound flank steak
1/2 pound mushrooms, sliced
2 tablespoons butter
2 tablespoons blue cheese
2 cloves garlic, crushed
Salt and black pepper, freshly ground to taste

❶ Select a flank steak that is thick enough to make a pocket (or
have your butcher make the pocket for you).

❷ Saute mushrooms until tender in 1 tablespoon butter. Add
cheese, remaining butter and garlic. Salt and pepper to taste.

❸ Fill the pocket with the mushroom-cheese mixture and close
with skewers.

❹ Salt and pepper steak and grill three inches from coals, until
done to your liking. Slice in diagonal slices against the grain.
Serve hot.

Makes 4 to 6 servings.

salsa verde

Italian green parsley sauce is a great dress-up for grilled or roasted meats and fish! Really good on Chicken Milanesa (see this section).

I slice day-old French bread
2 tablespoons red wine vinegar or lemon juice
1-1/2 cups flat-leaf parsley, chopped
2 tablespoons capers, with juice
2 cloves fresh garlic
I teaspoon Dijon mustard (optional)
3/4 cup olive oil
1/2 teaspoon salt
1/2 teaspoon black pepper, freshly ground

❶ In bowl of food processor, place bread, vinegar, parsley, capers, garlic and mustard. Add salt and pepper. Process until fully chopped.
❷ With motor running, slowly add oil.

Makes 1 cup.

Friends, they are kind to each other's hopes.
They cherish each other's dream.

Thoreau

peach tree
blackened seasoning

If you've tasted and enjoyed the Blackened Chicken on our Peach Tree Caesar Salad, you now have the secret to the great flavor that this seasoning mix adds—it is also delicious when used to season fish filets and shrimp.

1/4 cup thyme leaves, dried
1 tablespoon dill, dried
1/4 cup oregano leaves, dried
1/4 cup salt
1/2 cup paprika
2 tablespoons cayenne pepper
2 tablespoons dried parsley, crushed
2 tablespoons black pepper, freshly ground
1 tablespoon curry
2 tablespoons garlic powder
1/3 cup comino
1 tablespoon onion powder

Stir together and keep in air tight container.

Makes 2 cups.

NOTE:

THOROUGHLY COAT
BONED AND SKINNED
CHICKEN BREASTS,
FISH FILETS OR SHRIMP.
THIS CAN BE DONE
SEVERAL HOURS AHEAD
OF TIME AS WE DO IN
THE TEA ROOM. JUST
BEFORE SERVING, FRY
THE SEASONED MEATS IN
HOT OIL, TURNING ONCE
(I USE CANOLA) UNTIL
COOKED THOROUGHLY.
DELICIOUS AS THE
MAIN ENTREE, OR AS AN
ACCENT TO SALADS!

NOTE:

ENJOY THE GIFT OF

CREATIVITY WITH

THIS RECIPE. INSTEAD

OF THE DUXELLE FILLING

TRY ROASTED RED

PEPPERS AND GARLIC —

OR BLUE CHEESE AND

ROASTED GARLIC.

supper club celebration steak

Charles Schmidt and I are kindred spirits—he loves preparing feasts and serving others as much as I do! He is a dentist by profession but his wonderful talents have been savored by many in our community as he has lovingly given of himself in the foods he prepares for family, friends and charitable events. We've enjoyed this delicious steak many times in his home during our Supper Club days — and it's one that has been a definite favorite at our Hospital Gala Dinner.

6 8-ounce beef fillets
Salt and black pepper, freshly ground
12 sheets fillo dough
1 cup butter, melted
1-1/2 cups Duxelles (recipe follows)
1 recipe Mayonnaise-Mustard Sauce (recipe follows)

❶ Season steaks with salt and pepper. Butter baking sheets and place a sheet of fillo on plastic wrap. Brush fillo with melted butter. Top with another sheet of fillo and brush and butter.

❷ Place one fillet 3 inches from the narrow edge of fillo. Spread fillet with 1/4 cup Duxelles (recipe follows). Fold 3 inch flap of fillo over steak. Brush top and underside with butter.

❸ Fold in the long sides and brush with butter. Continue folding fillo around steak, buttering after each turn. Arrange seam side down on prepared baking sheet. Repeat with each steak.

❹ Bake in preheated 375 degree oven. Bake until pastry is puffed and golden - 20 to 30 minutes. Internal temperature should be 140 degrees for rare. Serve immediately with Mayonaisse-Mustard Sauce (recipe follows).

Duxelles:

2 tablespoons butter
2 tablespoons onion, chopped
1 teaspoon shallot, chopped
2 cups mushrooms, finely chopped (1/2 pound)
2 ounces smoked ham, chopped
1 tablespoon tomato paste
1/4 cup beef stock
1/4 cup Madeira wine
Salt and white pepper, freshly ground, to taste

❶ Melt butter, add onion and shallot and saute until translucent. Reduce heat.
❷ Add mushrooms and cook 5 minutes. Add ham and tomato paste and cook 5 more minutes. Reduce heat to low and add stock, Madeira, salt and pepper and cook. Stir frequently, until liquid has almost completely evaporated.

Mayonaisse-Mustard Sauce:

1 egg yolk
1 tablespoon fresh lemon juice
1 teaspoon Dijon mustard
Salt and white pepper
1/4 cup olive oil
1/4 cup vegetable oil

❶ Combine egg yolk, lemon juice, mustard, salt, pepper and 2 tablespoons oil in processor and mix until slightly thickened.
❷ With machine running, slowly drizzle remaining oils - until mixture thickens. Salt and pepper to taste.

Makes 6 servings.

Tina is so excited that we now have this recipe to publish in our cookbook. It brings back memories of when she and her brothers attended St. Mary's School. The Turkey Dinner is a traditional event well worth noting — a major family effort to raise money to support the school. When the children were young, I, along with many other parents, would take my roaster to the school cafeteria where I received a stuffed turkey to take home to bake slowly through the night. Early next morning, Hector would return the turkey so it could be sliced and served to an eager crowd of supporters. After waking up to the smell of turkey and dressing cooking in our kitchen, our mouths would water until we could get to the church for our lunch. Last year I understand that 4,000 people were served.

This example of community spirit is one of the very special ways that we who call Fredericksburg our home, are aware of our blessings.

This dressing has been used for many years by the families who settled in Fredericksburg and it is the same dressing served at this wonderful community event. Children love it because of its simple ingredients.

Be not forgetful to entertain strangers for thereby some have entertained angels unaware—

Heb. 13:2

sweets

edible flowers, flower confetti, and pretty green leaves...

I FIRST BEGAN TO LEARN ABOUT and use edible flowers in the early years of our Supper Club. Our dinners always centered around a chosen theme and on one particular evening we served a meal garnished with geraniums and begonias. We insisted that everyone must taste the flowers presented on his plate. It was a most interesting and memorable evening! Think back with me for a moment, and remember at that time, a garnish consisted of curly ruffled parsley, chopped chives and radish flowers!

Since that first introduction to the idea of using fresh flowers and herbs a whole world of opportunities has opened up for me to enjoy.

From the beginning days of our Tea Room, I have enjoyed presenting our desserts accompanied by a little flower. It has become a tradition for us, and now a plate that goes out without a flower doesn't look fully dressed!

When I cater a party or send out platters, I visit our gardens to gather little embellishments for the finishing touch. Fruit platters get sprigs of fresh mint and flowers. Vegetable platters are arranged on a bed of colorful kale, mustard leaves, swiss chard or lettuce greens. Sometimes I add a perfect sunflower bloom to the center and herb sprigs, or little herb and flower bouquets. Wedding cakes look so lovely when decorated "from the garden".

Equally as important to me are the leaves. This year, I planted giant red stemmed swiss chard in pots by my back door—the plant is pretty, and the leaves are close by when I need to line platters for my roasted vegetables. My garden collection of tiny ivy leaves is priceless—some of the leaves even have the shape of a heart—I love to use them when decorating cakes. The leaves of the scented geranium plants are lovely when using little ones with flowers or cakes, the larger ones for doilies under the cakes.

In my garden, I have a beautiful area lush with giant ivy leaves. The "ivy doilies" have become a trademark for us—we use them under "to-go" cakes, vegetables, and fruit. Their dark green color enhances the lovely culinary colors that we place on them.

Our gardens here at The Peach Tree have become an important source of the beautiful garnishing material that we use daily in our kitchens, and the stems that are arranged in the vases on our tables.

I love to visit Hill Country nurseries to search out new treasures to plant in the flower beds that surround our property. Our Texas climate is ideal for growing blooms throughout the year. During the cool months I like to grow pansies, johnny-jump-ups, nasturtiums and roses. The hot days of summer are perfect conditions for growing cosmos, coreopsis, sun-flowers, geraniums, and many, many others.

Early morning is always the most rewarding time to spend in the gar-den. Every morning is different—there are daily discoveries to be made as the baby foliage appears, and then the little flower buds. This year, my favorite has been the little clusters of flowers that suddenly appeared on my Italian parsley plants, looking like bursts of fireworks.

Children are very easily intrigued when introduced to the fun of gathering the edible flowers and using them to decorate.

On one occasion, I remember taking a salad to a pot luck dinner at a friend's home. Just before serving time, I tossed the salad with the dressing and sprinkled johnny-jump-ups over the top. The guests gathered around the table to pray and when we opened our eyes, the two little girls present had quietly gathered and eaten every flower from the salad!

When my granddaughters, Claire and Rose, visit, I like to walk them slowly through my garden so that I can introduce them to the different secrets that are hidden in the leaves in my herb garden. We pick off a leaf, enjoy the scent, and sometimes taste it, then move on to another plant. It's fun to bring some of our stems into the house for vases, and some to garnish our salads and dinner plates!

Flower confetti is one of the most effective ways to create a look of festivity and celebration. It is easily made by selecting flower petals and cutting them into very tiny pieces. It can be sprinkled over crostini, cold soups, salads, cup cakes, or cakes. A colorful finishing touch!

One year, I decorated Hector's birthday cake with a colorful mixture of yellows, oranges, blues, reds, pinks and purples. . .cosmos, bachelor buttons, geraniums, and begonias. It had the look of a Mexican fiesta cake!

An all yellow theme is happy looking! Pastel pink and blue (pansies are useful here) are a fun way to decorate for a baby shower. All red for a "Happy Birthday, Jesus" cake on Christmas eve. Pink and red for Valentines Day—and red and blue on a white frosted cake for the 4th of July!

FLOWER CONFETTI

Gather flowers from your garden and carefully remove the petals. With a very sharp cook's knife chop the petals into tiny confetti bits. This can also be done by stacking the petals, holding them securely between two fingers and cutting small slivers with a sharp pair of scissors. Use immediately or place in a covered container and keep refrigerated for one or two days.

fredericksburg peach pound cake

When Rhonda Smith worked for us in the office she brought a different cake to share each week. We asked her to repeat this one and then we asked for her recipe! Great recipes come from those who love to cook, and this one is special because we are always looking for new ways to enjoy our Hill Country peaches.

1 cup butter, softened
2 cups sugar
6 eggs, room temperature
1 teaspoon vanilla
1 teaspoon almond extract
3 cups flour
1/4 teaspoon baking soda
1/2 teaspoon salt
1/2 cup sour cream
2 cups ripe peaches, peeled and chopped

1. Preheat oven to 350 degrees.
2. Grease and flour 10-inch tube pan or bundt pan.
3. In large bowl, cream butter and sugar until light and fluffy.
4. Add eggs one at a time, beating well after each. Add vanilla and almond extract.
5. In small mixing bowl combine flour, baking soda, and salt. Add to creamed mixture.
6. Fold in sour cream and chopped peaches. Pour into prepared pan.
7. Bake for 1-1/4 to 1-1/2 hours, or until wooden toothpick comes out clean.
8. Top each slice of cake with sweetened whipped cream and a dash of cinnamon.

Makes 12 to 16 slices.

If you own **The Peach Tree Family Cookbook,** you
know how important the Collins Chocolate Cake recipe is to me
and my family. It symbolizes times of celebration — birthdays, Happy
Birthday Jesus cakes on Christmas Eve, and the reminder each time we enjoy
it we are part of one another — those present at the table those far away and
those who have gone to their eternal home with God — family sharing!

For a mother, one of the transitions we experience as our children grow up is
realizing that they won't always be home on their birthdays. Collins
Chocolate Cake has been the family birthday cake for us always. I would
send David and Carlos a Birthday Cake Kit when they lived away. It's
easy to send a cake through the mail unfrosted — the cake is
wrapped carefully — the frosting is packed in a separate
container — and be sure to include the candles
— when received the assembly is quick
and easy — and the precious
thread of a good tradition
unbroken!!

collins chocolate cake

4 ounces unsweetened baking chocolate
I cup butter or margarine
I cup brewed coffee
2 cups sugar
2/3 cup buttermilk
I teaspoon baking soda
2 eggs
I/2 teaspoon cinnamon
2 teaspoons vanilla
2 cups flour

❶ Combine chocolate, butter, coffee and sugar in bowl. Microwave 4 to 5 minutes, until melted.

❷ In 2-cup container, place buttermilk, eggs, cinnamon, vanilla and soda. Mix well and stir quickly into chocolate mixture.

❸ Stir in flour, blending well. Pour into 9 x 13-inch pan that has been greased and floured. Bake for 30 minutes in 350 degree pre-heated oven or until toothpick inserted in center comes out clean.

Frosting:
I/2 cup butter, softened
3/4 cup cocoa
3 cups powdered sugar
I teaspoon vanilla
I/4 cup brewed coffee

❶ Cream butter, add cocoa, blending well with food processor.

❷ Add powdered sugar and vanilla.

❸ Add coffee, a little at a time, until spreading consistency. Add more coffee, a few drops at a time if frosting is too thick.

Makes 12 servings.

NOTE:

THE INSTRUCTIONS I'VE

GIVEN HERE DESCRIBE

THE METHOD WE USE

WHEN WE MAKE THE

CAKE IN OUR TEA ROOM

KITCHEN. DONE THIS

WAY THE CAKE IS BOTH

EASY AND FAST. WE

MAKE MULTIPLE BATCHES

OF FROSTING —

SO NICE TO HAVE IN

THE REFRIGERATOR FOR

CAKES AND CUPCAKES.

pale yellow white cake

Sometimes, I'm asked to do a plain white cake, but they all look just too pale and unexciting! So here is my compromise — I feel it needs a little color! The result is a delicious tender cake just waiting to be embellished with many possibilities. The Tiramisu Cake (this section) is a delicious example of where you can take this recipe. There are no limits in the world of food — have fun and create!

3/4 cup butter
1/4 cup shortening
1-1/2 cups sugar
3 egg yolks
3 cups unbleached flour
1/2 teaspoon soda
1 teaspoon baking powder
1 cup buttermilk
2 teaspoons vanilla
5 to 6 egg whites
1/2 teaspoon salt

1. Preheat oven to 350 degrees.
2. In bowl, cream butter, shortening, sugar and egg yolks.
3. In separate bowl, mix flour, soda and baking powder. Add to butter mixture alternately with buttermilk. Beat well until smooth. Add vanilla.
4. Place egg whites and salt in bowl and beat until soft peaks form. Fold gently into cake batter.
5. Bake in 3 8-inch pans for 25 to 30 minutes. Cool 10 minutes, remove from pan and frost.

Makes 12 to 14 servings.

NOTE:

BUTTER CREME FROSTING

FOR THE FLOWER

CONFETTI CUPCAKES:

1/2 CUP BUTTER, DASH

OF SALT, 2-3 CUPS

POWDERED SUGAR, 1

TEASPOON VANILLA,

4-6 TABLESPOONS MILK.

BEAT ALL INGREDIENTS

EXCEPT MILK TOGETHER

UNTIL CREAMY. ADD

MILK, A LITTLE AT A TIME,

BEATING UNTIL LIGHT

AND FLUFFY.

love at first bite
chocolate cake

This is a dream of a dessert. Most of the preparation can be done early in the day, leaving the baking until just before serving. What's it like? The chocolaty pudding center collapses with the first spoonful, giving you two favorites in each bite — chocolate cake and pure chocolate pudding delight!

1/2 cup butter, softened
3/4 cup chocolate chips
1/4 cup unsweetened chocolate
4 eggs, whole
4 egg yolks
1/4 teaspoon salt
1/2 cup unbleached flour
1 cup powdered sugar
Granulated sugar for dusting

❶ Combine butter, chocolate chips and unsweetened chocolate in bowl. Melt in microwave.
❷ Place eggs and egg yolks together, in top of double boiler, whisking until heated.
❸ Add eggs to chocolate mixture and stir until smooth.
❹ Sift salt, flour and powdered sugar and add to chocolate-egg mixture. Mix well. Place in refrigerator until cool.
❺ Prepare ramekins with butter and dust with granulated sugar. Place 1/2 cup mixture in each ramekin.
❻ Bake in preheated 425 degree oven for 11 minutes.
❼ Invert on plate and serve with whipped cream and strawberry sauce or fresh strawberries.

Makes 4 or 5 servings.

tiramisu cake

I made this cake for Sherry Freeman, who wanted to celebrate her husband's birthday with his favorite dessert. He loves Tiramisu and this way he could have it all — cake, candles, and Tiramisu!

4 eggs, separated
1/4 cup Kahlua liqueur
1 pound marscapone cheese
1/2 cup sugar
1 recipe Pale Yellow White Cake (see this section), baked in
10-inch spring form cake pan
1/2 cup espresso
6 tablespoons semisweet chocolate, finely chopped

1. Mix together egg yolks, Kahlua, marscapone cheese and sugar and set aside.
2. Beat egg whites until frothy soft peaks form. Fold two mixtures together.
3. Cut Pale Yellow White Cake into three layers. Brush the top of each layer with espresso.
4. Put one layer back into the spring form pan and top with one third Tiramisu filling then one third of semi sweet chocolate. Repeat with each layer. Cover and refrigerate overnight for flavors to meld together and set the shape of the cake.
5. Remove cake from pan and place on serving plate.

Makes 12 to 15 servings.

venetian orange rum cake

2-1/2 cups unbleached flour
2 teaspoons baking powder
1 teaspoon soda
1/2 teaspoon salt
1 cup butter, softened
1 cup sugar
3 eggs
1 to 2 tablespoons orange zest
1 cup buttermilk or yogurt

1. Preheat oven to 350 degrees.
2. Combine flour, baking powder, soda and salt. Set aside.
3. With a mixer, beat butter on high speed until creamy. Add sugar gradually and continue beating until light and fluffy.
4. Change to medium speed and add eggs one at a time, beating well after each. Add orange zest and blend well.
5. Change to low speed and alternately beat in the dry ingredients and buttermilk, beginning and ending with the dry ingredients until just combined. Pour batter into 9-inch bundt pan that has been buttered (or prepared with non-stick spray).
6. Bake for 1 hour, or until wooden toothpick comes out clean.
7. Cool for 15 minutes, remove and glaze while still warm.

Glaze:
1/2 cup fresh orange juice
2 tablespoons fresh lemon juice
1/4 cup sugar
2 tablespoons rum

Combine juices, sugar and rum in sauce pan. Heat stirring until dissolved. Drizzle glaze over cake. Let set for 1 to 2 hours.

Makes 12 slices.

NOTE:

THIS CAKE MAKES A WONDERFUL GIFT BECAUSE IT KEEPS SO WELL. IT'S ACTUALLY BETTER IF EATEN THE NEXT DAY. I ALSO LIKE TO BAKE IT IN SMALL BUNDT PANS!

I LOVE CHOCOLATE AND ORANGE TOGETHER — THE CHOCOLATE GLAZE FOR CAKES AND COOKIES (SEE THIS SECTION) IS A DELICIOUS SPECIAL ADDITION, IF YOU LIKE!

GARNISH:
I LIKE TO USE CANDIED ORANGE PEEL.

Surprise!

Helana gave David a surprise birthday party the year they married, along with a picnic supper in their backyard. Carlos and his band were there for the entertainment. When it finally grew dark outside, Helana appeared with her own version of David's favorite dessert. Instead of his usual Chocolate Mousse, she had layered the mousse between multiple layers of chocolate cake shaped like a present, put a gold ribbon around it, added strawberries for color, and on top were 25 little skinny candles glowing brightly! What a beautiful night filled with treasured memories for our family!!

david's chocolate mousse birthday cake

Cake:
6 eggs, separated
1-1/4 cups sugar, divided use
3/4 cup flour, sifted
1/4 cup unsweetened cocoa
1/4 teaspoon salt
1 teaspoon vanilla
1 teaspoon water
1/4 cup sugar
1/4 cup brandy

1. Have all ingredients at room temperature.
2. Preheat oven to 350 degrees.
3. Using an electric mixer, beat egg whites until soft peaks form. Slowly add 1/2 cup sugar and beat until consistency of meringue.
4. Sift flour. Add cocoa and salt and sift again.
5. Beat egg yolks, add 3/4 cup sugar and vanilla. Add flour mixture and egg white mixture alternately to the egg yolks, folding carefully.
6. Pour batter into two 10-inch spring form cake pans. Bake for approximately 25 minutes. Remove from oven.
7. Mix together water, sugar and brandy. Stir until dissolved. Brush on warm cake layers.
8. Allow layers to cool completely and chill so they will slice easily.
9. Slice each layer in half to form 4 layers.

Layer Filling:
2-1/4 cups semisweet chocolate chips
1/3 cup strong brewed coffee
2 tablespoons raspberry liqueur
2 egg yolks
1/2 teaspoon vanilla
4 egg whites
Pinch of salt
1 cup heavy cream, chilled
2 tablespoons sugar

continued on next page...

❶ Combine chocolate chips and coffee in a heavy saucepan. Cook over low heat stirring constantly until chips are melted. Stir in liqueur. Remove from heat and cool to room temperature.

❷ Using a whisk, add egg yolks one at a time to chocolate mixture, beating thoroughly after each addition. Add vanilla.

❸ Beat egg whites with salt until stiff. In another bowl, beat the heavy cream until thickened. Gradually add the sugar, beating until stiff.

❹ Gently fold egg whites into the whipped cream. Stir about 1/3 of egg white-cream mixture into the chocolate mixture. Add remaining egg white-cream mixture. Blend thoroughly but gently.

❺ Put one layer back into spring form pan and top with one third of mousse. Repeat with each layer. Cover and refrigerate overnight for flavors to meld together and set the shape of the cake.

❻ Remove cake from spring form pan and place on serving plate. Spread with following topping.

Topping:
1-1/2 cups semisweet chocolate chips
1 cup heavy whipping cream

❶ Melt chocolate chips slowly.

❷ Pour melted chocolate into mixing bowl. Using whisk, pour whipping cream slowly into the chocolate. Continue to mix until smooth.

❸ Spread over the top of the cake or on the top and sides of cake.

Makes 12 to 14 servings.

margarita lime pie

Simply beautiful — and easy, too!

Crust:
1-1/4 cups graham cracker crumbs
1/4 cup sugar
1/4 cup chopped walnuts or pecans
1/4 cup melted butter

❶ Mix the crust ingredients thoroughly and press into bottom of a
   well-buttered 9 to 10-inch springform pan.
❷ Bake 15 minutes in a preheated 325 degree oven. Let cool.

Filling:
2 14-ounce cans condensed milk
4 egg yolks
1/2 cup fresh lime juice
2 tablespoons tequila

❶ Mix ingredients well and pour into baked pie shell. Bake in a
   300 degree oven for 12 to 15 minutes.
❷ Let cool before placing in refrigerator. Chill for several hours
   or overnight before serving.

Makes 12 servings.

NOTE:

GARNISH WITH WHIPPED
CREAM AND THIN SLICES
OF FRESH LIME AND
MINT SPRIGS. LIME ZEST
SPRINKLED OVER IS NICE,
TOO. ANOTHER IDEA —
GARNISH WITH FRESH
MANGO SLICES!

GARNISH:

SERVE WITH SLIGHTLY

SWEETENED WHIPPED

CREAM AND A FEW

FRESH RASPBERRIES OR

BLUEBERRIES

aunt nancy's lemon lush pie

My new friendship with Nancy Beal is another blessing from our son, David's marriage to Helana. Nancy is Helana's aunt, and with every visit we share food and entertaining ideas. She's another friend whose eyes sparkle when we talk about our love of cooking! This is her recipe from her own personal family cookbook. We made and served this pie in our Tea Room as soon as she sent me the recipe — it is often requested for our menu specials. I especially like to serve it garnished with fresh blueberries.

Crust:

1 cup vanilla wafers, crumbled
2/3 cup pecans, finely ground
1/4 cup sugar
1/4 cup butter, melted

❶ Preheat oven to 375 degrees.
❷ Combine all ingredients and pat into 10-inch pie plate.
❸ Bake for 8 minutes. Cool.

First layer:

1 8-ounce package cream cheese, softened
1/4 cup sugar
1/4 cup lemon juice, freshly squeezed

❶ Mix cream cheese with sugar and lemon juice until well blended and smooth.
❷ Place in cool pie shell and chill while making second layer.

Second layer:

1-1/2 cups milk

3/4 cup sugar

2 tablespoons cornstarch

2 egg yolks, well beaten

1/4 teaspoon salt

1 teaspoon vanilla

1/4 cup lemon juice, freshly squeezed

❶ Combine milk, sugar, cornstarch, egg yolks and salt in sauce pan
   and cook over very low heat. Stir constantly until thickened.

❷ Remove from heat and stir in lemon juice. Lay a piece of plastic
   wrap on the surface of mixture and cool.

❸ Spoon over cream cheese layer. Chill overnight if possible.

Makes 6 generous servings.

hill country fried pies

When I was growing up in the tiny town of Medina, Texas, there was the most wonderful little cafe owned by Mrs. Fee. She served a delicious lunch each day — something like meat loaf, potatoes, vegetables, homemade bread and pie for 75 cents. Sometimes she made apricot fried pies in the mornings. I can still remember the contentment I felt each time I captured one to eat. Since that time I've tried to duplicate it just as I remember. It's a rare treat for me now to indulge in a real fried pie — and just maybe the rarity is what keeps them special for me.

Pastry:
2 cups unbleached flour
2 teaspoons baking powder
1 teaspoon salt
1/2 cup shortening
1/3 cup ice water
1 recipe Apricot Kolache filling (see Breakfast)
Canola oil for frying - fill to 1/2 inch in pan

❶ Combine flour, baking powder, salt, shortening and ice water until well combined.
❷ Roll out pastry dough and cut into 6-inch rounds.
❸ Place 1/4 cup filling of your choice on each pastry round. Seal and fry in canola oil until golden.

Makes 6 or 7 pies.

NOTE:

THIS CAN BE REALLY EASY

IF YOU USE YOUR

FAVORITE PRESERVES —

OR JAM — OR PIE FILLING!

NOTE:

DO NOT USE GREEN

PEARS, THEY ARE TOO

HARD AND TOO DRY.

pear tart with sugary almond border

Another very special recipe from my friend, Charles. I love the sugary almond border that makes this wonderful tart rise to the sublime! The combination of pear and almond flavors is so good and elegant — impressive dessert!

Pastry:
1-1/2 cups flour
2 tablespoons sugar
1/4 teaspoon salt
1/4 teaspoon cloves
1/2 teaspoon grated lemon peel
1/4 pound cold unsalted butter cut in small pieces
1 egg yolk
5 tablespoons ice water

1. Butter a 10-inch tart pan.
2. Place dry ingredients and lemon peel in food processor fitted with metal blade. Process just to mix. Add butter, pulse until mixture resembles coarse meal.
3. Add egg yolk, pulse until blended. With machine running, quickly add ice water until mixture holds together. Form into ball, wrap in plastic wrap and chill for 1 hour.
4. Roll pastry out slightly larger than pan. Carefully lift pastry to pan and gently press against bottom and sides. Trim edges, prick bottom and sides with fork. Refrigerate half an hour.
5. Line pastry-filled pan with foil, pressing it gently against pastry. Fill with uncooked dried beans or rice so crust doesn't bubble. Bake 15 minutes in a preheated 375 degree oven.
6. Remove from oven, take out liner and beans. Return crust to oven for an additional 5 minutes. Cool on rack.

Glaze:

1/4 cup apricot preserves

2 tablespoons Amaretto Liqueur

1 teaspoon almond extract

❶ Heat preserves, liqueur and almond extract over low heat, stirring. Strain mixture.

❷ Brush tart shell with 2 tablespoons glaze. Reserve remainder.

Filling:

1/2 cup finely ground almonds

1/2 cup sugar

1 tablespoon flour

6 large (or 9 small) firm ripe Anjou pears, peeled, halved lengthwise and cored.

❶ Stir ground almonds, sugar and flour; sprinkle over glazed shell.

❷ Slice pear halves crosswise. Place slices in circle over almond mixture in shell. Fill spaces between slices with remaining pears. Return tart to oven for 20 minutes.

Sugary Almond Border:

1 egg white

1 cup sliced almonds

1/2 cup sugar

1/4 teaspoon salt

1/4 teaspoon cinnamon

❶ Beat egg white to froth. Add almonds, sugar, salt and cinnamon.

❷ Spoon sugary almond mixture around edge of the tart. Return to the oven an additional 20 minutes. Remove from oven, brush with remaining warm glaze. Serve at room temperature.

Makes 8 servings.

apple guide

Do you find yourself being confused when deciding which apples to buy for your apple desserts? I have — and this has led me to research and make my own little apple guide.

I hope this is helpful to you. With so many varieties available to us in the market it is good to know how to use them to your best advantage.

All apples cook differently, and lend different qualities to the dishes we prepare. For instance, when making apple sauce we want a softer texture with lots of flavor, whereas for pies and cobblers we want an apple that will hold together with firmer texture.

Some of their other interesting qualities is whether they are tangy, or sweet - buttery or spicy.

Becoming familiar with these qualities can lead to fun and give you an opportunity for creativity. You may want to make a pie with two kinds of apples, one for texture - one for flavor.

My favorite apple for tarts and cobblers is the Granny Smith. It remains firm and I like its tart, fresh apple flavor very much.

FIRM APPLES – great for pies, cobblers, tarts
   Granny Smith, Gala, Fuji, Golden Delicious

SOFTER APPLES – for apple sauce and apple butter
   McIntosh, Jonagold, Rome Beauty

BUTTERY FLAVOR
   Fuji, Gala, Golden Delicious, Jonathan

SPICY FLAVOR
   Gala, Braeburn

apple cobbler with sugar cookie crust

We have served this over and over for special occasions in the Tea Room and it is always a favorite. Each time I make it I think of another variation — to give it a different twist!

Filling:
9 apples, Granny Smith, sliced, unpeeled
Juice of 1/2 lemon
Zest of 1 lemon
1/2 cup sugar

1. Preheat oven to 350 degrees.
2. Mix together ingredients and put in 9 x 13-inch baking dish.

Crust:
1 cup butter, melted
1 cup sugar
1 large egg
1-1/2 cups unbleached flour
1 teaspoon baking powder
1/4 teaspoon salt
1 teaspoon vanilla

1. In large mixing bowl, cream butter, sugar and egg.
2. Sift flour, baking powder and salt together in separate bowl.
3. Combine flour mixture, vanilla and creamed butter mixture.
4. Using a spoon, drop large dollops of batter over the apples, leaving spaces in between.
5. Bake for 40 minutes or until golden brown.

Makes 10 to 12 servings.

NOTES:

ADD 1 CUP DRIED CRANBERRIES TO APPLE MIXTURE FOR CRANBERRY APPLE COBBLER WITH SUGAR COOKIE CRUST.

INSTEAD OF APPLES, USE 9 CUPS PEACHES IN FILLING RECIPE AND ADD 1/2 TEASPOON CINNAMON AND 1 TEASPOON ALMOND EXTRACT. NOW YOU HAVE PEACH COBBLER WITH SUGAR COOKIE CRUST!

NOTE:

THIS MAKES ONE TART TO

SERVE 8 PEOPLE.

INDIVIDUAL TARTS CAN

BE MADE BY CUTTING

THE DOUGH INTO 6 INCH

CIRCLES. PLACE 1/4 TO 1/3

CUP OF APPLE FILLING

AND BRING UP SIDES

CRIMPING TOGETHER TO

HOLD FILLING.

apple tartlet

There was a time when I thought that if it were dessert — it had to be chocolate. Lately I find that if given a choice of a great pastry with apples — that is what I choose. I'm ever hopeful that the pastry will be tender and flaky, and the apples still warm — and when it is — it's true comfort food!

The following recipe is my new favorite dessert. The more often I prepare it, the more variations I dream up! What makes this recipe such a treat is the tender flaky pastry topped with tender, just cooked apples - not overly sweetened, not overcooked - delicious and uncomplicated, not overworked!

I like the light crunch that the addition of cornmeal gives this pastry. Be careful not to over mix and you will be rewarded with a tender and flaky crust.

Pastry:
2 cups unbleached flour
1/2 teaspoon salt
1 tablespoon cornmeal, optional
1-3/4 sticks butter
1/4 cup ice water, maybe 1 to 2 tablespoons more
3 tablespoons sugar

❶ Mix flour, salt, and optional cornmeal in bowl. Cut in butter with a pastry blender until texture is consistency of cornmeal with pea size lumps throughout.

❷ Add ice water, mixing with a fork, or rubber pastry spatula until blended. Place dough into plastic bag and gently press into a flat disk. Place in refrigerator for an hour or overnight.

3. Roll dough to 12 inch circle, 1/4 inch thick. Place on ungreased baking sheet.
4. Place prepared fruit in center of dough, mounding toward the center.
5. Raise edges of dough to enclose the fruit, gently pinch the pleats of the dough together to hold the sides together.
6. Sprinkle the top lightly with sugar. Bake for 20 to 25 minutes or until crust is golden and fruit is bubbly. Serve warm.

Filling:

3 to 4 apples, Granny Smith or Empire, peeled and sliced
1 tablespoon fresh lemon juice
3 tablespoons sugar

1. Place apples, lemon juice and sugar in mixing bowl, mix well.
2. Place in prepared pastry.

Streusel topping:

1/4 cup sugar
1/4 cup unbleached flour
3 tablespoons butter

1. Place flour and sugar in mixing bowl. Add butter and cut into mixture until well mixed and crumbly. Sprinkle over surface of apples in the pastry.
2. Place in a preheated 425 degree oven and bake 20 to 25 minutes or until the crust is golden and the fruit is bubbly. Serve warm. Serve with a spoonful of Maple Créme Fräiche or Ginger Whipped Cream (both recipes in this section).

Makes 8 servings.

NOTE:

THIS RECIPE WILL GIVE YOU A DELICIOUS APPLE TART. I LIKE THE RUSTIC APPEARANCE. YOU CAN CHANGE IT BY SOAKING DRIED CRANBERRIES, GOLDEN RAISINS OR APRICOTS IN BRANDY AND ADDING THEM TO THE APPLE MIXTURE. SPRINKLE LIGHTLY TOASTED ALMONDS, PUMPKIN SEEDS OR PINE NUTS WITH MAPLE SUGAR ON TOP BEFORE BAKING.

skillet oatmeal cookies

Tina treasures this recipe given to her by Lacy Gilbert. Lacy only allows pure and natural foods in her kitchen — note that these cookies are made with maple syrup and whole wheat flour, no sugar.

2-1/2 cups rolled oats
3/4 cup butter
3/4 cup whole wheat pastry flour
1/2 teaspoon salt
1/2 teaspoon baking powder
3/4 cup maple syrup
1 egg
2 teaspoons vanilla extract

❶ Preheat oven to 350 degrees.
❷ Brown oats with butter in iron skillet.
❸ Mix browned oats, flour, salt and baking powder and set aside.
❹ Mix syrup, egg and vanilla. Add dry ingredients and mix well.
❺ Drop dough by tablespoonfuls on a cookie sheet prepared with non-stick spray.
❻ Bake 12 to 15 minutes or until golden brown.

Makes 2 dozen cookies.

apricot jam strudel

I get into big trouble when I make this delicious pastry because I can't resist the temptation to eat more than I should! My neighbor, Joan Tatum shared the recipe with me because she knows how much I like apricots.

Pastry:
3/4 cup butter
2 cups flour
8 ounces sour cream

❶ Cut butter into flour until it resembles course meal.
❷ Stir in sour cream. Divide into 4 portions and chill several hours.

Filling:
1 18-ounce jar apricot preserves or jam
4 ounces flaked coconut
1 cup pecans, chopped

❶ Roll out each portion of pastry on a floured board into the shape of a rectangle (7 x 12 inches). On each pastry, spread 1/4 of the jar of apricot jam very thinly and sprinkle with 1/4 of coconut and 1/4 of pecans.
❷ Roll up jelly roll fashion, turn ends under.
❸ Bake 45 minutes at 375 degrees. Sprinkle with powdered sugar before serving.

Makes 4 to 6 servings

sugar cookies

For decorating this is my new favorite sugar cookie. Just a little more baking powder makes it even more tender than the one in the first cookbook. We use this recipe to make our decorated cut out cookies. It makes a nice thick cookie... just as good to look at as it is to eat!

5 cups unbleached flour
4 teaspoons baking powder
1-1/2 teaspoons salt
2 cups sugar
1 cup butter, softened
4 eggs
Zest of 1 lemon (1 tablespoon)
2 teaspoons vanilla
1 teaspoon almond extract

1. Place flour, baking powder and salt together in mixing bowl. Set aside.
2. Place sugar and butter in food processor. Process until mixture is creamy. Add eggs, lemon zest, vanilla, almond extract and process until blended.
3. Add flour mixture and pulse just until dry ingredients are incorporated.
4. Place dough in plastic bag. Pat into a flat disk and refrigerate for about 2 hours.
5. On a lightly floured board, roll out one third of dough at a time. Roll to about 1/8 inch thickness and cut out with cookie cutters. Put shapes on greased baking sheets and bake in preheated 400 degree oven for 10 minutes. Do not allow to brown. Cool on racks.

Makes 32 cookies (2-1/2 inches in diameter).

Busy little hands making cookies—

royal icing

Ann Surma worked as our Tea Room hostess for many years. Before moving to Fredericksburg, Ann and her husband owned and operated a family bakery. She created many little works of art from the sugar cookies that we baked to sell in our deli. This is the recipe for icing that she gave us and we have found it works very nicely for us.

2 large egg whites, or more to thin icing
4 cups sifted powdered sugar, or more to thicken icing
Juice of 1 lemon

Beat egg whites until stiff but not dry. Add sugar and lemon juice. Beat for 1 minute more.

a proper tea, indeed

MY IMPRESSION OF TEA TIME USED TO BE ONE of stuffiness and bland flavors. I envisioned ladies sitting in a parlor in stiff straight chairs and wearing rigid corsets — nothing to which I could relate! In looking closer, I see this is not the case after all. There are as many options and opportunities to present a proper tea as the creative mind can imagine!

Tea can be served in the most elegant silk upholstered parlor, or in the middle of a Texas pasture! The menu can take hours of preparation, or when pretending with little people - maybe two minutes. To me, it is an attitude of a time set apart to share and rest with those we love - those with whom we want to renew or begin relationship - and sometimes it is time spent with oneself - time set apart to reflect and renew.

LITTLE THINGS NOTES:

Little things are very important to me

— I love details —

little vases all in a row — Johnny jump ups

Butter in a heart dish with flowers   Smiles

Bread served on my beautiful hand carved heart board

"Cynthia, there are no little things."
                    My Mother

NOTE:

TURN THESE INTO JAM

TARTS BY USING YOUR

FAVORITE FLAVORS OF

JAM IN PLACE OF THE

TOPPING.

little lemon shortcakes

These are so so easy! And just as good to eat — For special occasions, garnish each one with a fresh berry or a tiny edible flower — I use johnny jump-ups in the spring!

1/2 pound butter, softened
1-1/3 cups unbleached flour
3/4 cup powdered sugar
1/2 cup cornstarch
1/2 teaspoon almond extract
1/2 teaspoon vanilla

❶ Preheat oven to 350 degrees.
❷ In a small bowl, cream the butter.
❸ Combine flour, powdered sugar, cornstarch, almond extract and vanilla with butter.
❹ Spray mini muffin pans with non stick spray. Spoon dough into muffin pans and bake for 15 minutes until golden brown. Let stand for 10 minutes.
❺ Make small indentations in each shortcake with thumb print or handle of wooden spoon. Let cool, then gently remove from pans.

Topping:
1/2 cup Lemon Curd
1/4 cup cream cheese, softened
Garnish: Sprinkles of lemon zest, fresh berries, edible flowers

❶ Stir together ingredients until smooth.
❷ Lightly dust with additional sugar and fill each shortcake with 1 teaspoon of topping.

Makes 30 shortcakes.

N O T E :

BISCOTTI CAN BE STORED

IN AN AIRTIGHT CONTAIN-

ER FOR AT LEAST 1 MONTH.

orange almond biscotti

My friend, JP, makes the best Biscotti I've ever tasted. He sometimes made them for us to sell in the Deli when he was Tea Room manager. Here is his version of this tasty Sicilian style cookie — so good with an afternoon cup of coffee.

2 cups unbleached white flour
1 teaspoon baking powder
1/4 teaspoon salt
4 tablespoons butter
1 cup granulated white sugar
2 large eggs
1/2 teaspoon vanilla extract
1/4 teaspoon almond extract
3/4 cup almonds (with skins), toasted, chopped
2 tablespoons orange zest, minced

❶ Sift first 3 ingredients together in a small bowl.

❷ Beat butter and sugar in a large bowl until light and smooth. Add eggs one at a time, then add extracts. Stir in almonds and zest. Sift dry ingredients over batter, then fold into dough until just mixed. Do not over mix!

❸ Adjust oven rack to middle position and heat to 350 degrees. Halve dough and turn each portion onto an oiled cookie sheet covered with parchment. Dough will be sticky!

❹ Using floured hands, quickly stretch each portion of dough into a rough 13 x 2-inch log, placing them about 3 inches apart on the sheet. Pat each dough shape to smooth it. Bake, turning pan once, until loaves are golden brown and just beginning to crack on top, about 35 minutes.

⑤ Cool the loaves for 10 minutes. Lower the oven temperature to
   325 degrees.
⑥ Cut each loaf diagonally into 3/8 inch slices with a serrated
   knife. Lay the slices about 1/2 inch apart on the sheet, cut side
   up, and return them to the oven. Bake, turning over each cookie halfway through baking, until crisp and golden brown
   on both sides, about 15 minutes. Transfer to wire rack and
   cool completely.

Makes 3 to 4 dozen.

chocolate glaze
for cakes and cookies

So easy — and so good! There are many ways to use this chocolate
glaze — it's a nice filling between cake layers, or spread on top for
an overall chocolate glaze finish. We also use it to fill our Chocolate
Filled Peanut Butter Cups (see this section).

3/4 cup semi sweet chocolate chips
1/4 cup heavy cream

❶ Place chocolate and cream in small mixing bowl. Microwave on
   low for 4 to 6 minutes until chocolate is melted. Stir until
   smooth and glossy.
❷ Spread on cake while glaze is warm. Let cool until set.

Makes 3/4 cups.

N O T E :

MAKE A CHOCOLATE

GANACHE TART — BAKE

YOUR FAVORITE TART

CRUST — SPREAD A

DOUBLE RECIPE OF THIS

GLAZE OVER CRUST, LET

COOL — AND FILL WITH

FRESH FRUIT SUCH AS

STRAWBERRIES,

CHERRIES, RASPBERRIES,

BLUEBERRIES. TOP

WITH WHIPPED CREAM

OR CRÉME FRÂICHE

(SEE THIS SECTION) IF

YOU LIKE!

JOHN PHELPS AND I

NAMED THESE COOKIES

WHEN WE STARTED SERV-

ING THEM IN OUR TEA

ROOM. I DON'T KNOW

WHY, BUT THIS NAME

JUST SEEMED TO FIT! WE

MAKE THEM BIG TO SELL

IN THE TEA ROOM — BUT

THEY CAN BE MADE TINY

AS WELL. EVERY BITE IS

PURE CHOCOLATE

DELIGHT!

WE MAKE MULTIPLE

BATCHES OF THESE COOK-

IES — KEEP THEM ON

TRAYS IN THE COOLER —

THEN BAKE THEM — AS

THE DEMAND REQUIRES

— WHICH, BY THE WAY,

IS MOST OFTEN!

mud dobbers

Yes! These are the cookies you've been waiting for! They are a Tea Room favorite. Some of our customers buy them by the dozen.

4 ounces unsweetened chocolate
12 ounces semisweet chocolate
1 pound unsalted butter
1/2 cup unbleached flour, sifted
1/2 teaspoon baking powder
1 teaspoon salt
4 large eggs
1-1/2 cups sugar
4 teaspoons powdered (not granular) instant coffee
4 teaspoons vanilla extract
12 ounces semisweet chocolate morsels (2 cups)
4 cups walnuts, broken into large pieces

1. Preheat oven to 350 degrees. Prepare cookie sheets with cooking spray.
2. Melt unsweetened chocolate, semisweet chocolate and butter in top of small double boiler. Cook covered for a few minutes. Stir and set aside to cool slightly.
3. Sift flour, baking powder and salt. Set aside.
4. Beat eggs, sugar, coffee and vanilla at high speed for a minute or two. Beat in melted chocolates and butter on low speed just to mix. Add dry ingredients and beat just to mix.
5. Stir in chocolate morsels and walnuts.
6. Refrigerate for 2 to 3 hours.
7. Use 1/3 cup dough for each cookie. Place on baking sheets two inches apart. Bake 16 or 17 minutes - no longer. The cookies may appear to be soft, but that's part of what makes them so good.

Makes 16 to 18 cookies.

brown sugar brownies

Tina asked Ellen Hill to share this family recipe with her because it's the kind of brownie that makes you want to pick them up by the fist-full. Ellen's a great cook. She used to make these brownies for her brothers and sister who would gobble a whole pan in one afternoon. Now she's making them for her family, one of a wealth of recipes she will pass on to her children.

1 pound brown sugar
1 cup butter
2 eggs
2 cups sifted flour
1 teaspoon baking powder
1/2 teaspoon salt

1. Preheat oven to 350 degrees.
2. Place sugar and butter in double boiler over hot water and cook until sugar is dissolved. Let cool.
3. Add eggs one at a time beating thoroughly. Stir in remaining ingredients and spread into ungreased pan (15-1/2 x 10-1/2 inch).
4. Bake for 25 minutes. Cut into 2 inch squares.

Makes 15 to 20 squares.

bread pudding

IT'S A CHALLENGE FOR ME TO WRITE DOWN OUR BREAD pudding recipes. As soon as we begin to prepare a bread pudding in the Tea Room, up pops another ingredient to inspire us! For those of you who frequent our Tea Room, I know you understand what I'm saying. If you check out our dessert list you'll see such titles as Leah's Cookie Bread Pudding - Peach Tree Brownie Bread Pudding - Lemon Poppy Seed Bread Pudding - and on goes the list!

Bread Pudding has become a natural for us because of the easy access that we have to our delicious left-over breads, baked daily in our kitchen. And when Lydia and I begin to plan a bread pudding we are delighted if there happen to be a few croissants available to us!

Following is the basic recipe we use to begin our bread pudding. Keep in mind that there are many directions you can go with this dessert. Layers of leftover cake, cookies, fruits, or jams all can add a different twist to this basic recipe, as well as the flavors you can incorporate into the custard such as vanilla, coconut, almond, or lemon.

And texture, by adding toasted walnuts, pecans, or almonds can be layered into the bread layers - or sprinkled on top - sometimes BOTH!!

The most important thing to remember - after you've chosen your ingredients, is the amount of custard you will need to make your pudding light and tender. We prepare ours the evening before it is to be baked. It has all night to soak up the custard, then we add more just before placing it into the oven. We've also baked it on the same day with the bread having 1 to 2 hours soaking time. This will work fine if your ingredients are not overly dense.

Following is a list of some successful combinations that we've done in our kitchen. Let your creativity take flight from these ideas!

LAYER BREAD, APPLE WALNUT CAKE, MORE BREAD, top with brown sugar and toasted walnuts, cinnamon and nutmeg - serve with whiskey sauce and a sprinkle of chopped walnuts.

LAYER BREAD, SWEET POTATO PINE NUT BREAD, GOLDEN RAISINS, MORE BREAD - top with brown sugar and a little butter. Serve with custard sauce and a drizzle of Cajeta and sprinkle with toasted pine nuts.

LAYER BREAD, LEFTOVER LEMON GINGER BARS (if you can capture them before they're eaten), croissants - top with brown sugar and almonds and little butter - serve with custard sauce or a dollop of Lemon Curd.

LAYER BREAD, CHOCOLATE CHIP OR OATMEAL COOKIES, RAISINS, AND PECANS - serve with custard sauce and a drizzle of Chocolate Sauce.

LAYER CROISSANTS, APRICOT OR PEACH JAM AND TOASTED ALMONDS OR ALMOND PASTE - more croissants, sprinkle top with sliced toasted almonds and maple sugar.

The **BASIC BREAD PUDDING** recipe follows on the next page.

basic bread pudding

10 to 15 1-inch slices of day old French bread (preferably home-made) or 1/2 French Bread and 1/2 croissants, sliced
1/2 cup butter, room temperature
8 eggs, beaten
1 cup granulated sugar
8 cups milk
2 tablespoons vanilla
Brown sugar
Nutmeg

1. Layer bread slices in buttered 11 x 13-inch baking dish.
2. Combine eggs, sugar, milk, and vanilla. Mix together with a whisk. This step can also be done in the blender.
3. Pour mixture over layered bread. The bread may not absorb all the liquid. Save the extra egg-milk mixture. Refrigerate for 4 hours or overnight. Add the reserved liquid.
4. Sprinkle bread pudding generously with brown sugar and nutmeg. Bake in a preheated 325 to 350 degree oven for one hour until pudding is puffed and golden, and knife inserted in center comes out clean. Serve warm or at room temperature with Custard Sauce or Whiskey Sauce (see Sweets).

Makes 15 servings.

almond toffee

Sally and I began our friendship when our children were very young. When she and her husband bought a house in the country, they and their two little boys actually moved into our house and we lived together for two months while their house was being remodeled. The memories of the adventure of our two families living together in our small house are treasured by Sally and me.

During the Christmas holidays Sally makes toffee for us and brings it in a basket tied with lovely paper and ribbons. The toffee is tender, crunchy, buttery and all covered with chocolate!

1 cup butter
1-1/3 cups sugar
3 tablespoons water
1 tablespoon light corn syrup
1 cup almonds, blanched, toasted and coarsely chopped
4 to 4-1/2 ounce chocolate bar, melted
1 cup almonds, blanched, toasted and finely chopped

1. Melt butter, then add sugar, water and corn syrup. Cook to 300 degrees — stirring constantly (use candy thermometer).
2. Quickly stir in coarsely chopped almonds and pour into a well greased 9 x 13-inch pan.
3. Cool thoroughly. Turn onto waxed paper. Spread top with half of melted chocolate. Then spread half of the finely chopped almonds on top.
4. Let cool and cover with waxed paper and turn over.
5. Spread the bottom side with remaining chocolate and nuts.
6. Leave until hardened and break into bite sized pieces.

Makes 10 to 12 servings depending how generous you are!

NOTE:

WE'RE EXCITED THAT JAY

BLACKBURN, OUR FOOD

SERVICE MANAGER,

HAS COME TO JOIN OUR

PEACH TREE FAMILY. HIS

TALENTS ARE MANY,

ESPECIALLY SINCE HE IS A

FABULOUS BAKER. THIS

IS A RECIPE THAT HE

SHARED WITH US TO SELL

IN THE TEA ROOM —

EVERYONE BECAME

ADDICTED FROM THE

FIRST BATCH!

lemon ginger bars

Crust:

2/3 cup powdered sugar

Dash of salt

2 cups flour

I tablespoon ground ginger

I cup unsalted butter, softened, cut in chunks

❶ Sift together powdered sugar, salt, flour and ginger. Combine and blend with butter. Press into greased 9 x 11-inch pan.

❷ Bake in a preheated 350 degree oven for 15 to 20 minutes, until light brown.

Filling:

4 eggs, beaten

2 cups sugar

2/3 cup flour

I teaspoon baking powder

Juice of 3 lemons (6 tablespoons)

Zest of 3 lemons

5 dashes of Angostura bitters

I/2 teaspoon cream of tartar

Powdered sugar to sprinkle on top

❶ Whisk together eggs and sugar until slightly frothy. Add lemon juice, bitters and lemon zest.

❷ Sift together flour, baking powder and cream of tartar. Combine with egg mixture.

❸ Pour on slightly cooled crust.

❹ Bake at 350 degrees for 25 to 35 minutes or until top is uniformly light brown.

❺ Sprinkle powdered sugar on top. Cut into squares.

Makes 12 to 15 squares.

bordeaux prunes

Charles served this to us one evening when Hector and I dropped in for a visit. He just happened to have it in his refrigerator — it's a wonderful kind of dessert that you can put together and enjoy when your heart desires!

2 pounds pitted prunes
1 bottle Bordeaux wine
3/4 cup sugar
1/2 vanilla bean, split

❶ Plump prunes in 1/2 bottle wine for 6 hours. Cover dish.

❷ Simmer prunes, wine (including remainder of bottle), sugar and vanilla bean over low heat for 20 minutes. Remove from heat and cool. Serve cold or at room temperature garnished with a dollop of Créme Frâiche.

Makes 8 servings.

SARAH SAWTELLE MAKES

THE CHOCOLATE SAUCE

(SEE THIS SECTION) TO

TOP OFF HER MOTHER'S

ICE CREAM — SUCH A

TREAT!

summer sunday
vanilla ice cream

Kathryn Sawtelle lives in a grand old farm house surrounded by beautiful gardens and yards. When her large family gathers at her home on summer Sundays, she mixes up this ice cream custard and lets her strong grandchildren churn it by hand the old fashioned way — one sits on the churn while the other cranks — memories in the making!

4 eggs
2 cups sugar
1 can condensed milk
Pinch of salt
2 tablespoons vanilla
10 cups milk or half and half or all cream

❶ Beat eggs well, add sugar and salt, beat again.
❷ Add condensed milk and vanilla. Mix thoroughly, then add enough milk or cream to fill 6-quart ice cream freezer.

Makes 6 quarts.

chocolate sauce

NOTE:

MAY BE REHEATED OVER

HOT WATER OR GENTLY

IN THE MICROWAVE.

Tina, who has fond memories of Sunday afternoons outside the
Sawtelle home in Boerne, asked Sarah Sawtelle for her Chocolate
Sauce recipe. Her mother's Summer Sunday Vanilla Ice Cream and
this Chocolate Sauce are hard to beat in the heat — or anytime!
The sauce is so delicious that it's great to have in the refrigerator —
ready to use and a real temptation to eat by the spoonful.

1/4 cup butter
1/4 cup unsweetened chocolate
1/2 cup cocoa
3/4 cup sugar
1/2 cup cream
1/4 teaspoon salt
1 teaspoon vanilla

1. In a small saucepan over low heat, stir together butter and
   chocolate until smooth.
2. Add cocoa, sugar, cream and salt and bring to boiling point.
3. Remove from heat and add vanilla.

Makes 1-1/2 cups.

NOTES:

YOU MAY KEEP THE

CUSTARD SAUCE IN THE

REFRIGERATOR FOR

SEVERAL DAYS.

PLEASE KEEP IN MIND

THAT YOUR MICROWAVE

MAY COOK DIFFERENTLY

FROM MINE. THE POINT

IS TO END UP WITH A

CUSTARD THAT IS THICK

AND SMOOTH.

custard sauce

Lydia and I developed this technique for making custard in our
Tea Room kitchen. It was inspired by our ever demanding need for
saving (or finding) TIME! Here the microwave is doing the work
and we (now you) are spared having to stand at the stove stirring —
it's been a great time-saver for us!

4 cups milk or light cream
4 eggs
3/4 cup sugar
1 tablespoon unbleached flour
2 teaspoons vanilla

Heat all ingredients except vanilla in microwave for 7 minutes.
Whisk — microwave 5 minutes — whisk — microwave 5 more
minutes — whisk — then add vanilla — whisk until smooth.

Makes 4 cups.

lemon curd

This is basically the Peach Tree Lemon Sauce recipe from our first cookbook. I just added more egg so it will be thicker for spreading. Lemon Curd is available in specialty food markets, but it's very easy and satisfying to make your own.

1/2 cup butter
5 eggs
2 cups sugar
3/4 cup orange juice
Zest and juice of 1 lemon
1 tablespoon cornstarch

❶ Melt butter in non-aluminum saucepan on low heat.
❷ Using a blender or food processor, blend eggs, sugar, orange juice, lemon juice, and cornstarch. Add to melted butter and cook on low heat, stirring constantly. Cook until mixture is thick and bubbly, about 8 minutes.
❸ Remove from heat and add lemon zest. Serve warm or cold.

Makes about 2 cups.

❤ NOTE:

LEMON CURD KEEPS

WELL IN YOUR

REFRIGERATOR — AND

IS NICE TO HAVE ON

HAND FOR QUICK AND

EASY DESSERTS AND

TEA PARTIES!

NOTE:

WILL KEEP INDEFINITELY

IN THE REFRIGERATOR.

dessert whiskey sauce

This recipe is from Jane West. It's wonderful on bread pudding and pound cakes. It's fun to watch people take a bite. First there is a smile and an "UMM." And then they ask for the recipe.

1 cup butter
2 cups sugar
1 egg, beaten
1/2 cup whipping cream
1/4 cup bourbon, or to taste

❶ Cream butter and sugar. Add the egg and cream. Heat in double boiler until everything is melted together and egg is cooked. Add bourbon and stir.
❷ Serve immediately or make ahead and reheat to serve.

Makes 4 1/2 cups.

NOTE:

GREAT TOPPING FOR

DESSERTS — TRY IT ON

THE APPLE TARTLET —

SEE THIS SECTION!

ginger whipped cream

1 cup whipping cream or heavy cream
2 tablespoons sugar
1/4 cup sour cream
1 tablespoon rum or brandy
1/4 teaspoon ground ginger or 2 tablespoons fresh grated ginger

❶ With an electric mixer, whip cream, sugar and sour cream to form soft peaks.
❷ Add rum or brandy and ginger and beat just until stiff.

Makes 1 cup.

maple créme frâiche

Delicious topping for apple and peach cobblers, dessert crepes and breakfast waffles. I like it "not too sweet," but you can add more maple syrup if you wish!

1 cup whipping cream
3 tablespoons buttermilk
2 to 3 tablespoons maple syrup

❶ Pour cream into a glass container and stir in the buttermilk.
❷ Cover the mixture and place in a draft-free area of your kitchen.
❸ Do not disturb for 8 to 12 hours when mixture will be thick and the consistency of sour cream. Stir in maple syrup right before serving. Store in refrigerator.

Makes 1 cup.

NOTE:

IF YOU DELETE MAPLE SYRUP IN THIS RECIPE, IT BECOMES OUR TRADITIONAL PEACH TREE CRÉME FRÂICHE — SIMPLE DELICIOUS GARNISH FOR DESSERTS AND SOUPS!

zinfandel strawberry sauce

2 cups sliced strawberries
1/2 cup sugar
1/2 cup red wine - zinfandel or something fruity
1 teaspoon balsamic vinegar (optional)

Place in saucepan and bring to boil. Lower to medium heat and cook about 10 minutes. Can leave chunky or puree as you desire! Serve hot or cold.

Makes 2-1/2 cups.

NOTE:

A BEAUTIFUL SAUCE TO SERVE WITH FRESH FRUIT, POUND CAKE, ICE CREAM —AND WOULDN'T IT BE GOOD ON PANCAKES! BALSAMIC VINEGAR IS NOT CRITICAL TO THIS RECIPE - IT JUST ENHANCES THE FLAVOR OF THE STRAWBERRIES.

Peach Tree Family

Evelyn Geistweidt bakes all of the beautiful cakes and cheesecakes that we serve daily in our Tea Room. We have enjoyed developing recipes together during most of the 14 years since opening the doors of our Peach Tree Tea Room. For a two year period of time, when Evelyn was not baking with us at the Peach Tree, the back baking kitchen was still lovingly referred to as "Evelyn's" kitchen. We're very proud of this cheesecake. It's a nice light tasting dessert — and the tropical flavors taste really good in the summertime.

pineapple coconut cheesecake

GARNISH:

SLICED MANGOS,

TOASTED COCONUT

Crust:

1 cup flaked coconut, toasted

1/2 cup ground pecans

2 tablespoons melted butter

Toast coconut in 350 degree oven for 10 minutes or until golden.
Mix with other ingredients and press into 9-inch springform pan.
Set aside.

Filling:

5 8-ounce cream cheese

1 cup sugar

1 teaspoon vanilla

1/3 cup milk

1 cup cream of coconut

1 teaspoon almond extract

5 eggs

1 cup drained crushed pineapple

1 cup flaked coconut

1/4 cup rum

❶ Cream together cream cheese, sugar, vanilla. Add milk, cream of
coconut, almond extract and eggs, stirring after each addition.

❷ Add pineapple, coconut and rum - stirring to mix thoroughly.

❸ Pour filling into crust. Bake for 1 hour in preheated 300 degree
oven. Turn off oven and let cheesecake cool in oven with door
closed for several hours or overnight. Refrigerate.

Makes 14 to 16 servings.

tembleque

When Hector and I lived in Puerto Rico, Tembleque was a dessert that we enjoyed at the local restaurants. It's very refreshing — just a light finish at the end of a hearty meal. The Puerto Ricans served it unmolded with a cinnamon sprinkle — that's very good, plain and simple. It's also nice with a garnish of tropical fruit such as mango slices or fresh pineapple and maybe a light drizzle of rum.

3 cups unsweetened canned coconut milk
1/2 cup sugar
1/4 cup corn starch
1 tablespoon gelatin, softened in 3 tablespoons water

GARNISH:

GROUND CINNAMON, OR

FRESH TROPICAL FRUIT

❶ In a food processor or blender, place coconut milk, sugar, and corn starch. Blend well to combine.

❷ Place in saucepan, heat to a boil, stirring constantly until custard coats a spoon, 4 to 5 minutes.

❸ Add softened gelatin, and stir to combine.

❹ Pour into a 4 cup mold or bowl, or 6 small custard cups. Cover surface with plastic wrap to prevent a skin from forming. Place in refrigerator until firm, 2 or 3 hours or overnight.

❺ When ready to serve, unmold on a plate and garnish with a sprinkle of cinnamon or fresh fruit.

Makes 4 to 6 servings.

index

250

notes

notes

Management and Leadership in Nursing and Health Care

An Experiential Approach

Second Edition

Elaine La Monica Rigolosi, EdD, JD, FAAN

SPRINGER PUBLISHING COMPANY

NEW YORK

Springer Publishing Company, Inc.
11 West 42nd Street
New York, NY 10036-8002

Acquisitions Editor: Ruth Chasek
Production Editor: Pamela Lankas
Cover design by Joanne Honigman

06 07 08 09/ 5 4 3 2

Library of Congress Cataloging-in-Publication Data

Rigolosi, Elaine La Monica, 1944–
  Management and leadership in nursing and health care : an experiential approach / Elaine La Monica Rigolosi.—2nd ed.
    p. ; cm — (Springer series on nursing management and leadership)
  Prev. ed.: Nursing leadership and management. Monterey, Calif. : Wadsworth Health Sciences Division. c1983
  Includes bibliographical references and index.
  ISBN 0-8261-2525-5
  1. Nursing services—Administration. 2. Health services administration. 3. Leadership.
  [DNLM: 1. Nurse Administrators. 2. Administrative Personnel. 3. Leadership. 4. Nursing Care—organization & administration. WY 105 R572m 2005] I. Rigolosi, Elaine La Monica, 1944– Nursing leadership and management. II. Title. III. Series.
RT89.L3 2005
362.17'3'068–dc22   2004025462

Printed in the United States of America by Bang Printing.

To my most treasured friend . . .
My husband, Robert S. Rigolosi

Feeling . . . Speaking
Silent . . . Laughing
Hurting . . . Healing
Serene . . . Smiling
Alone . . . Together

Always with me . . . .

Elaine La Monica Rigolosi